Dr. Cleland Boyd McAfee

was born in 1866 and died in 1944. He was educated at Park College and at Union Theological Seminary. After teaching mental and moral philosophy at Park College for thirteen years, he served successive pastorates in Chicago and Brooklyn before joining the faculty of McCormick Theological Seminary in 1912. He was Moderator of the General Assembly in 1929, and Secretary of the Presbyterian Board of Foreign Missions, 1931-1936. And he wrote many books.

© Harris & Ewing

Katharine McAfee Parker

is one of Dr. McAfee's three daughters. She was educated at Vassar College, and she has written magazine articles. Her great institutional love is Hanover College, where her husband, Dr. Albert G. Parker, Jr., has been president for twenty-four years. Mrs. Parker was on the first National Council of Presbyterian Women, and she has served for twelve years on the Presbyterian Board of Foreign Missions. She has four children and seven grandchildren.

NEAR TO THE HEART OF GOD

Near to the
Heart of God

THE BOBBS-MERRILL COMPANY, INC.
INDIANAPOLIS • NEW YORK

Near to the Heart of God

BY

CLELAND BOYD McAFEE

AND

KATHARINE McAFEE PARKER

THE BOBBS-MERRILL COMPANY, INC.

PUBLISHERS

INDIANAPOLIS • NEW YORK

CONTENTS

CONTENTS—*Continued*

PART I

CLELAND BOYD MCAFEE

1866-1944

by

KATHARINE McAFEE PARKER

For my mother, with love,
and because she had so
large a part in my father's
life and ministry

NEAR TO THE HEART OF GOD.

C. B. McA.

CLELAND B. McAFEE.

1. There is a place of qui - et rest, Near to the heart of God,
2. There is a place of com - fort sweet, Near to the heart of God,
3. There is a place of full re - lease, Near to the heart of God,

A place where sin can - not mo - lest, Near to the heart of God.
A place where we our Sav - iour meet, Near to the heart of God.
A place where all is joy and peace, Near to the heart of God.

REFRAIN.

O Je - sus, blest Re - deem - er, Sent from the heart of God,

Hold us, who wait be - fore Thee, Near to the heart of God.

CLELAND BOYD McAFEE

1866-1944

MY FATHER was a preacher and a teacher and a board secretary and a writer. He liked to play the piano in any appropriate key, and with a good strong bass, so that people could sing hymns. He wrote a score of books and innumerable articles and tracts. He traveled and lectured around the world, was moderator of the Presbyterian General Assembly, and left his mark on many ministers who were his students in McCormick Theological Seminary.

But he will probably be remembered longest for a little song he wrote when he was still a very young man.

> There is a place of quiet rest,
> Near to the heart of God;
> A place where sin cannot molest,
> Near to the heart of God.
>
> O Jesus, blest Redeemer,
> Sent from the heart of God,
> Hold us who wait before thee,
> Near to the heart of God.

9

There is a place of comfort sweet,
Near to the heart of God;
A place where we our Saviour meet,
Near to the heart of God.

There is a place of full release,
Near to the heart of God;
A place where all is joy and peace
Near to the heart of God.

The song was born out of tragedy and suffering and faith, and
this is how it happened:

My father's father, John Armstrong McAfee, was one of the
founders and the first president of Park College in Missouri. In
the late years of the past century his five sons (Lowell, Howard,
Lapsley, Cleland, Ernest) and his only daughter (Helen) were
all living in Parkville, serving the college. My father was the college preacher and director of the choir, and it was his custom,
when communion services came, to write the words and music of
a response which his choir could sing and which would fit into
the theme of his sermon.

One terrible week, just before a communion Sunday, the two
little daughters of my Uncle Howard and Aunt Lucy McAfee
died of diphtheria within twenty-four hours of each other. The
college family and town were stricken with grief. My father
often told us how he sat long and late thinking of what could be
said in word and song on the coming Sunday which would comfort and strengthen all the sorrowing hearts.

"I knew I could not say that we *understood* what had hap-
pened," he told us. "We cannot understand the *mind* of God.
We cannot understand His reason for letting such tragedy come.
But we can understand His *heart*. We can trust His love what-

ever happens, and we can find peace and comfort always if we stay near to the heart of God."

So he wrote the little song. The choir learned it at the regular Saturday-night rehearsal, and afterward they went to the Howard McAfees' home and sang it as they stood under the sky outside the darkened, quarantined house.

It was sung again on Sunday morning at the communion service, and then for most people it slipped away into the memory of the tragic days of sorrow and was almost forgotten.

But when my Uncle Lapsley left Parkville and became the pastor of the First Presbyterian Church in Berkeley, California, he took the song with him, taught it to his people and used it regularly in the Sunday-morning service. It spread from there, not only to the church life of the West Coast but also around the world, for the First Presbyterian Church of Berkeley has long been ardently missionary-minded, and the many young people who went from it as missionaries kept on singing "Near to the Heart of God" wherever they went.

When my father and mother went around the world in 1925 they heard it sung in every mission land they visited. Sometimes the people knew my father had written it, sometimes not. Once in China my father rose to bow his acknowledgment after a group of schoolgirls had sung his song, and the principal was pleased that he had enjoyed it. "We don't know where it came from," she explained. "Someone found it somewhere and taught it to the girls, and we sing it often." My father was happy to tell the girls that they had just sung the song for its author and composer, and he bowed again to their prolonged applause.

"Near to the Heart of God" is in many books of sacred songs. It has been used widely on radio programs, and many church choirs and groups sing it often.

My father delighted to point out how timely and how timeless true Christian faith is. The song which he wrote is an example of the Now and the Forever. It had great meaning when a group of college students sang it outside a saddened home in a small Missouri town. In all the years since then it has had meaning, too, where it was sung in any tongue, for its simple and profound message is forever and everywhere true.

There is a like meaning and message of timeliness and timelessness in my father's own faith and life.

His faith in God, the Father, Son, and Holy Spirit grew and deepened with the lengthening of his days on earth, but he never had to change it to meet the changing scenes and demands of his life. The abiding Christian truths by which he lived when his ministry began were the same with which it ended in this part of life.

His first book was a tiny volume, published in 1899, entitled *Where He Is*. It was on immortality and in it he wrote:

How like Jesus it is to make companionship the chief attraction of Heaven! ... We are to be where He is. ... And He will be where we are until that time. ... You remember that great verse of promise wherein Jesus says, "Lo, I am with you always." Well, just before it He said, "All power is given unto Me." As though He would say: "I know the work I give you is too much for you; I know the life I offer is too hard for you; I know the service I demand is too great for you; but look to Me! I have all authority. I can bid your foes depart or submit. Since all power is Mine and you need Me so much, I am with you always!"

After more than fifty years of preaching and living his faith, my father had had much more experience with human need and divine power than when he wrote those words, but his confi-

12

dence in the presence and the nearness of his Master was the same.

His ministry began on the campus of Park College. After graduation from the college in 1884 at the age of eighteen, and later from Union Theological Seminary in New York, he returned to Park, not only as preacher in the college church and director of the choir but also as Professor of Mental and Moral Philosophy and as leader of campus prayers at six o'clock every weekday morning without fail. He kept an eye on the printing shop, too, because he had worked there as a student. He had traces of printer's ink in his blood for the rest of his life.

He also had time to court and marry my mother, then called Hattie Brown. (She became Harriet as the Maggies became Margarets, the Jennies Janes, and the Katies Catherines or Katherines or Catharines or Katharines or even Kathryns.)

My father went at his courting with characteristic assurance. Hattie Brown, also a Park College graduate in the class of 1888, was teaching Latin in the Park College academy. She says that "of course" she greatly admired young Professor Cleland, "as everyone did," but she had no idea at all that he was "interested" in her. So she was taken by surprise when he invited her to go with him on Thanksgiving Day of 1891 to a country home where he was to perform a marriage ceremony. He called for her with a horse and buggy and away they went for a nice long ride and very pleasant conversation, returning from the wedding in time for a strawberry festival at Number One, the main college building.

A few days later, on December seventh, to be exact, he walked home with her from a Christian Endeavor social. She was particularly glad to accept his invitation because she had been afraid that she might have to walk home with one of her several beaux whom she wished to avoid. As my father said good night to her at the gate of the house where she was rooming, he asked whether she would be at home the following evening. My mother says she simply does not know *what* struck her at that moment, or *how* she knew, but she suddenly knew beyond a doubt *what* he wanted to say to her. She walked sedately into the house, but once inside she was so excited that she really tore around "like a wild woman" and dashed upstairs to tell her roommate (a cousin of Cleland's) what he had said. The roommate took it very calmly. She wasn't at all surprised, she said with a smile. My mother could have shaken her.

The next evening finally arrived, and so did my father. Hattie took him into the parlor and made it easy for him to come to the point. When he asked her to marry him she said, Yes. She has felt a little embarrassed ever since that she took no time to "think it over," but she was as forthright as he was assured, and they settled the matter without delay.

They were married the following August tenth in Hattie's home church in Girard, Kansas. (She escaped being an "old maid" by a narrow margin. Her twenty-fifth birthday was just three days after the wedding.) There being, obviously, no sufferers from hay fever in the immediate family, the church was lavishly decorated with goldenrod, which was available without cost in almost every community where their anniversary was subsequently celebrated.

For more than sixty years since my mother took my father for better, for worse, for richer, for poorer, she has held to the conviction that he was one of the best things the Lord ever made. He felt exactly the same way about her. He gave her the first copy of his first book and wrote on the flyleaf:

> E'en heaven of Christ would lose
>   for me its joy,
> Did I not know that "Where He Is"
>   there thou shalt be;
> And this I know since where
>   *thou* art here in the earth
> I catch the clearest vision
>   of the Christ of Galilee.

C.B.M.

5 Nov. 1899

They spent fifty-two years together on earth, companions of each other's hearts and minds.

My father never doubted that his work was important, not in itself but as part of the large plan of God. My mother was equally convinced of it and she did every earthly thing she could to free him for the service of the Lord. She saw that his meals came on the table regularly and that he ate them; that his suits were pressed, his socks mended, his shirt collars clean. Even on their Golden Wedding Day in Jaffrey, New Hampshire, in 1942, he counted on my mother to tell him when to get dressed for the party. She always picked out his ties, and ran the bank account, and brought up the children, and of course entertained his relatives when they came to visit.

When he was studying or writing she handled everything but dire emergencies and she was the final judge of whether they were sufficiently dire to bring to my father's attention. He didn't have to seem ungracious or preoccupied, for my mother applied a rule of her own life to other people: "Mr. McAfee is busy now and cannot be disturbed." Once, just once, she had a sick headache on the maid's day out, and asked my father to heat a little water for some tea. But it was too much of an ordeal for him. After that, she had her headaches when the maid was in.

My father liked to read to her what he had written, and he wanted her in the congregation every time he preached or spoke. She listened intently and was ready with an answer when he asked his invariable question on the way home: "Well . . . how did it go?" She knew very well how it had gone, and she told him, both when "it was good" and when "it was not so good." She encouraged him endlessly but never failed to correct any faulty mannerisms of speech or idea which he might have picked up.

My mother did considerable church work herself and is well remembered for her clear head and keen organizational ability. But her chosen career was my father. His work was their work and they both knew it.

The years since his death in 1944 have been very lonely for her, but she is grateful every day that he went on ahead of her to heaven because she knows he would have found earth difficult without her care, and she can wait for the day when she will join him forever.

Their three daughters were born in Parkville. The youngest, Mildred, was born in 1900, which has always made it easy to remember how old she is, and to calculate from that how old I, Katharine, am (perennially three and a half years older) and how old Ruth is (three and a half years older than I am). Each of us was named Cleland before we were born, but we all turned out to be girls.

The Forty-first Street Presbyterian Church of Chicago called my father away from Parkville in 1901. On the first Sunday he preached there he was warned that the service might be disturbed by loud and ominous noises outside the church. He was not to be alarmed, one of the elders said. It would be one of the new "horseless carriages" roaring up the boulevard. My father was quite sure he could preach through anything, and he did. As a matter of fact, his message was never broken or interrupted by scientific discoveries or new ways of living. He had no fear that something might turn up one day which would make God less powerful or explain Him away. My father could be concerned about the way people might use knowledge and power, but he was never nervous lest they learn something God didn't intend them to know or that would take away their need of Him.

Three happy years in the church on Grand Boulevard in Chicago and then eight years in Brooklyn in the great Lafayette Avenue Presbyterian Church put a lasting stamp of the pastor on my father. He was scholar enough to be called back to McCormick Theological Seminary in Chicago in 1912 to be Professor of Didactic and Polemic Theology—a title which I learned to say smoothly and use effectively with my teen-age friends and which I was sorry to see dropped in favor of the still incomprehensible but much less impressive one of Systematic Theology. But whatever the title, my father was always a pastor as well as a teacher to the "boys" in his classes in theology, or missions, or literature, or ministerial practices.

He wanted them to learn a faith they could live and give for the rest of their days. They remember how he bade them lay aside their notebooks when he spoke of the meaning of the cross. They remember how clearly he worded their difficulties and how patiently he led them through their doubts. They remember how earnestly he spoke to them of the workings and problems and opportunities of the church, in America and around the world.

They remember that he cared about anything which might aid or hinder them in their ministry, including their manners, their dress, their grammar, their haircuts, and the way they managed their money. He scattered practical advice through his lectures. Such as this:

Now, Gentlemen, a week will come, after you are in your own churches, when the Lord leads you in the preparation of an unusually fine sermon for the next Sunday. You will know it is the best sermon you ever had, and you will hardly be able to wait for Saturday to come and go, so it will be Sunday morning and time to go into your pulpit. But when you wake up on Sunday it will be pouring down rain, a veritable deluge. You will go to church and find only a faithful few who will have dared to come out in such weather. You will be terribly tempted to keep your good sermon for another day and a larger congregation, and to pull something out of your head for the little flock who sit before you on the stormy morning. But don't, I beg you, put off the good sermon. The people who came out in the rain deserve better than your very best effort. See that you give them at least your best. And if you do, the Lord will arrange to give you another idea by the next Sunday.

McCormick men remember the Sunday afternoons they spent in our home on Chalmers Place when my father played the piano for them to sing.

"Turn to Number 45," he would say. " 'The day Thou gavest, Lord, is ended . . .' And note particularly the second stanza:

'We thank Thee that Thy Church unsleeping
While earth rolls onward into light,
Through all the world her watch is keeping
And rests not now by day or night.'

18

Give thanks every day, Gentlemen, that you are engaged in so great a task!"

He sang familiar hymns with them and taught them others that they did not know. "A hymn is not good just because it is old, or just because it is new," he said. "The church needs both. People talk about liking only the old hymns, forgetting that the ones they call old had to be new once upon a time. When you are sure a hymn is a good hymn, even if it is new or little known, don't be afraid to use it."

We remember when he taught the men to sing "an old but unfamiliar hymn":

> Not so in haste, my heart!
> Have faith in God and wait;
> Although He linger long,
> He never comes too late.
>
> He never comes too late;
> He knoweth what is best;
> Vex not thyself in vain;
> Until He cometh, rest.
>
> Until He cometh, rest,
> Nor grudge the hours that roll;
> The feet that wait for God
> Are soonest at the goal.
>
> Are soonest at the goal
> That is not gained by speed;
> Then hold thee still, my heart,
> For I shall wait His lead.

"Now this is a simple little melody," my father said, "and the words are simple—you will note that the last line of one stanza is the first line of the next—but it has a fine depth of meaning and a lesson we all need to learn and relearn."

He commented on most of the hymns before the boys sang them. "My good friend William Pierson Merrill wrote this: 'Rise up, O men of God, Have done with lesser things.' It is sure to have a permanent place among the hymns of the church. . . . 'A mighty fortress is our God': This is Martin Luther's great hymn. Never sing it without thinking how the Lord used him. . . . 'Make me a captive, Lord, and then I shall be free': Put that idea into a sermon sometime. . . . 'O Christ, forget not them who stand, Thy vanguard in the distant land': Sing this today with special thought of the Christians in China."

After the students had sung a dozen or more hymns of his choosing or theirs, my mother served them tea from bottomless pots, and sandwiches and cheese-on-crackers from an endless supply. When We Girls were at home and helped her make the sandwiches we fussed at her for going to so much trouble over them." The Boys don't care what they eat so long as it is plenty," we said. "They don't appreciate all this daintiness." She paid us no heed. "I want it nice," she said, cutting off crusts. "These boys are not only lonesome and hungry right now. They are also learning to be ministers and are going out into churches. Some of them definitely need training in holding a plate with a teacup and a sandwich on it and talking at the same time." We noticed that some of them seldom reached the point of talking.

My father kept up with many of his boys by letters and visits and prayers after they left the seminary. They counted on him for interest in everything they did and for wise counsel in their problems.

One of them likes to tell of what my father did for him at a time when he was discouraged about his church and himself and was seriously considering leaving the ministry altogether. He saw my father at a meeting of the Presbyterian General Assembly, told him how he was feeling and asked if he could talk with him about other work he might go into. They made an appointment to have lunch together, and when the young preacher arrived at the place of meeting he found Dr. Robert E. Speer with my father. "You won't mind, will you," my father asked, "if Dr. Speer has luncheon with us? Then we can talk about your personal problem later." The preacher, now no longer young, never forgets the conversation around that table as Dr. Speer and my father talked of the church and the world. They spoke of India and the Philippine Islands as though they had just been there. They discussed soberly the need of a new building for a school in Brazil. They smiled over some missionary's experience with a new language. They spoke of great plans for the near future. They made the task of the church seem big and exciting and needing the help of every follower of Christ. It had its discouraging aspects, of course, but they were only part of the greatest business in the world.

Dr. Speer left soon after lunch, and my father turned to the young man. "Now, let's see," he said. "What was it you wanted to talk to me about?"

"I guess it wasn't important," the young man said. "At least it doesn't seem important now."

My father put his arm around his shoulder, and with an affectionate twinkle in his eye he said, "Give my regards to your wife, and God bless you in your work!"

Many honors came to my father. None ever touched him more than the honor of having his boys, all over the world, preaching and teaching and living the Faith he knew was eternal. The year he was moderator of the Presbyterian General Assembly and traveled all over the country, he stood with special joy in the pulpits of the churches where his own boys were the pastors.

Ruth and I each married our favorite one of our father's students. Quite early in life Ruth had decided, and announced, that she would never marry (1) a minister or (2) a man with a common name, but she dropped both ideas when the Reverend George William Brown walked into her life and stayed. Reverend Albert George Parker, Jr., and I were married on my mother's and father's twenty-eighth wedding anniversary. Mildred was a bridesmaid but did not catch onto the values of marriage for herself until exactly twenty-five years later when she married Reverend Douglas Horton. Not that she was idle in the meantime. She was president of Wellesley College for thirteen years and head of the WAVES during World War II, and the perfect aunt for her Brown and Parker nephews (2) and nieces (5).

When Mildred went to Wellesley and joined the near-by Congregational Church, a friend of my Grandfather McAfee wrote a very strong letter to my father to ask *what* a *McAfee* was doing in the *Congregational* Church, and what did *my* father think *his* father was thinking in heaven to learn that one of his grandchildren was no longer a *Presbyterian?* My father enjoyed quoting the gist of what he said in reply to the gentleman's letter:

The gates of heaven are surely not set up alphabetically according to denominations, and if, by any chance, there is one gate for Congregationalists, another for Presbyterians, and so on, a grandfather could certainly wait at any of the gates to welcome a granddaughter coming in. Once inside, we can be sure there

22

will be only one large family in the Father's House and King-dom!

We are sure our father rejoices now in heaven that his two grandsons are ministers (Presbyterian) and three of his grand-daughters are ministers' wives (2 Presbyterian, 1 Congrega-tional). We are equally sure he is just as pleased over the grand-daughter whose husband is a professor of economics and the one whose husband is a civil engineer. "It isn't a man's vocation that determines his worth to the world," he said emphatically, "but the spirit and purpose of his life."

The fullest, richest chapter of my father's life was spent at McCormick Seminary, where he and my mother lived and taught for nineteen years, but it was right and proper that, for the five years (1931-1936) before he retired, he was a secretary of the Presbyterian Board of Foreign Missions.

As far back as he could remember he had had a passion for foreign missions. "The Christian Faith is a World Faith," he said. "Christ's teachings can't be true anywhere unless they are true everywhere." My father was sure that Jesus meant exactly what He said when He told His disciples to go into all the world telling sinful, needy men of His loving, saving power. The command was for all His disciples in every generation. My father was continuously grateful that he could have a part in obeying that command. God might have made a Plan for telling the Good News without using people as witnesses. But He didn't. His Plan needed witnesses in Jerusalem (their own community) and in all Judea (their state) and Samaria (their country) and unto the uttermost part of the earth. "This is made perfectly clear in the first chapter of Acts, the eighth verse," my father would say.

God had put the life of every Christian in a large setting. Every disciple had his place in the whole task. My father said it over and over like this:

> Our own lives are small at their greatest
> and short at their longest,
> but they can be part of something
> as wide as the world,
> and eternal,
> if we give them to God
> to use in building His Kingdom.

In Platte Presbytery, in his Missouri days, my father was chairman of the foreign-missions committee. He was a member of the Presbyterian Board of Foreign Missions for many years. In 1925 he was the first recipient of the Joseph Cook lectureship which took him to "the principal cities of India, China, Japan" and to Syria, Thailand and Korea, to "state and defend the Christian faith" and to visit the mission lands he had known and loved so long.

Everywhere he went, in any season, any country, any situation, he was full of peace and excitement. There was a good light in his eyes and a joy in his voice. The light was not there because he saw no darkness; the joy was not there because he saw no suffering. He knew the needs and sins of the world. All the more reason then to rejoice in the Hope of the world. He was not afraid to offer his Master, and his Master's service, to anyone. In the lectures he gave in Asia he never left out the paragraph in which he said:

We who have been Christians for generations do not ask that others copy us. We offer them the Original whom we have poorly copied. We do not want them to drink from our stream.

We offer them the Fountain out of which our stream has flowed, and which is not responsible for the impurities we have cast into it. We do not want them to take our teaching. We offer them our Teacher who is also our Saviour, and ask them to sit at His feet. We do not want the world to come to us, but to Him.

Even to a ten-year-old daughter he was convincing when he preached on foreign missions. On a certain Sunday in Brooklyn I was so stirred by his sermon that when the offering plate came around I put my entire allowance for the week into it, literally giving, as he had suggested, "all I had." In honesty I must report, however, that the spell of my father's words had worn off by the time I went, after the service, to his office where the kindly deacons let me help them count the offering each week. I took back a little change, to get me through to my next allowance, hoping the Lord would understand that I would try to reimburse Him later. Maybe I straightened it out with Him by marrying a missionary and going with him to China.

My father was very happy to have missionaries in his family. They would miss me at home, he assured me, but they would be very proud that now the family was serving the cause of Christ on two continents. "China does not seem far away to your mother and me," he wrote, "because it is part of God's Kingdom and near to His heart. When you and we are near Him, we will not be far from each other."

My father was using familiar language and he was in a familiar place when he moved into an office at 156 Fifth Avenue, New York City, and began his work on the staff of the Presbyterian Board of Foreign Missions. He was given the "portfolio" covering Korea, Japan, the Philippines and Thailand, but there was no part of the church's work in any part of the world that was not on his heart and mind. His office was easy to get into, and he listened well. He dealt with problems in terms of people, and with today in terms of eternity. He was never a secretary with a portfolio, but always a pastor with a people.

To the missionaries in Korea in 1935 he wrote a pastoral letter:

Our Lord does come graciously to every complicated condition of our lives and offers us an alternative: peace for our disquiet, faith for our fear, trust for our anxiety—something beautiful to put over against every disturbing thing in our lives. We have much occasion to think of it in these times when there are disturbances all around us, and we realize that Christ means to set our feet upon a rock and to establish our goings. Our one concern is to be sure that we have got His alternative and accepted it with full hearts. May God give all of you every alternative which you need.

My father took hold of the problems of people where the people themselves were concerned about them, and he was never afraid of honest questions anywhere in the world or about anything.

The head of a school he had visited in China wrote him to say that the girls who had heard him speak wanted him to tell them where they could best find the answers to many questions they had about becoming Christians. He wrote back:

Please express to the girls, when you have occasion, the assurance of one of their older brethren in America that the best answer to a great many questions is to set out to follow Christ, and the answers are found along the way. One cannot wait to have the answers before following, because we walk by faith and not by sight and the wisest man must sometimes let questions wait.

My sister Ruth remembers a letter she wrote to my father

when she was in college. She sent it to him with some misgiving. "I think you ought to know," she wrote, "that I don't know what I believe any more. I have begun to question a lot of things about God and Christ and the Bible and what people ought to do. I'm not sure of anything. I'm sorry to tell you this, but you ought to know it." By return mail my father replied, "Your letter has come and it makes me very happy. This is the first time I have seen any evidence that you were really *thinking* about anything. Go right ahead. Study and learn and think as much as you can. In the end you will have a deeper faith and understanding for using all of your mind." Ruth remembers that she was a little disappointed that he was not alarmed about her "faith."

My father had a great way, too, of bringing encouragement to people who were discouraged and of renewing hope and zest in tired hearts. While he was lecturing in India a missionary wrote a letter home about his visit at an annual meeting where the group had been wishing they might have "somebody from the outside who could give us a new supply of inspiration." The letter went on:

God knew we needed it, so He sent us straight from Heaven and from the Middle West and from McCormick Seminary the nicest, inspiringest blessing you can imagine, in the shape of Dr. McAfee. . . . He came right into our next to the last day's business session, looking so nice and gray-and-pink-and-white and friendly and so understandingly human that everybody took a fresh breath of the refreshing breeze he brought in. That afternoon he just listened. That evening he addressed a non-Christian audience. Then he came back to us in the evening and made us laugh and lift up our heads and go at our task again with a new sense of the bigness of it.

27

The next morning he came back and listened to reports for an hour. Then he talked to us about the things folks don't always dare to say out loud: about theology and where we stand, and where we are going, and what matters, and how to make men know and feel and get the great experience and the sense of the victory of Jesus Christ. . . . He preached at the big Marathi Church in the afternoon, and then led a communion service afterwards, when he spoke of "The Meaning of the Cross" until we went away with the hushed sense of having found the strength to meet our needs. . . . We're too apt to see only our own corner of the job, and we need to touch, sometimes, at closer range, the thoughts of big men in big business—the world business of Christ's Church.

My father never really retired. As long as he lived he went to several churches each year, often where a former student was the minister. Sometimes he spent several weeks in one church, leading Bible Study classes, speaking on the Christian Faith, playing and interpreting hymns, putting new heart into the pastor, talking with laymen, urging a large view of life on young and old and middle-aged.

He preached his last sermon on Sunday, January 23, 1944, in the Episcopalian Church in Asheville, North Carolina. That evening, at Sunnyside Inn where he and my mother were living that winter, he sat down at the piano, as was his custom, and played hymns and sang with the group which gathered. At the close of the evening he turned around on the piano bench and spoke informally about church union, one of the unfinished tasks on earth in which he was deeply concerned and at which he was always working.

One morning in the hospital, after the operation from which he did not recover, he spoke of the long watches of the night, and the comfort of Bible verses, and especially the new meaning

he saw in "long suffering . . . meekness . . . peace." "I must
preach a sermon about that," he said.

On his desk were notes of sermons he expected to preach and
articles he intended to write. In early February, out of days still
full of plans and promises of helpful ministry, he stepped across
into the heaven he knew would seem like home.

> He had no fear of death
> For life to him was life that knows no end:
> Some years on earth
> Then on to further service
> With his Lord.
>
> He had no fear for us who stay on earth:
> He knew that near the heart of God
> There would be comfort, joy, and peace.
> And, too, he knew that we—
> His family,
> His boys who preach the Word,
> His friends of every race and age and clime—
> Would go on working
> At the task he loved
> Far more than life itself:
> The task of helping build on earth
> The Kingdom of our God.

PART II

EDITORIALS

by

CLELAND BOYD McAFEE

written 1912-1916 for

The Continent

A PRESBYTERIAN CHURCH WEEKLY

published

1910-1926

by

THE McCORMICK PUBLISHING COMPANY

CHICAGO

ABOUT THE EDITORIALS . . .

AT EVERY STAGE of my father's career he was writing "something that needed to be said," in words as honest and simple as possible. He wrote about the Christian faith, the Bible, the foreign-mission enterprise. He wrote books, Sunday-school lessons, articles, tracts, book reviews. (His book *The Ruling Elder, His Duties and Opportunities* is still an official book in The Presbyterian Church in the U.S.A.)

While he was a professor at McCormick Theological Seminary he wrote the editorials which appeared first in *The Continent* and are here reprinted. We all remember how rapidly he wrote them. He had a few moments, and a few notes on the back of an envelope, and with a few fingers he tapped out his thoughts on the typewriter and mailed off the copy. They are like letters a pastor might write to his people about problems they were talking about and facing together. The editorials sound the way my father talked and they represent the essence of his spirit and faith.

They appeared originally one-a-week. They might stand one-a-day reading, but they are not to be taken in one dose, like a whole bottle of vitamin pills at once.

Forty years ago my father sat in his study in Chicago and wrote these editorials. They were timely then and they are timely now, for they speak of the need of men and the power and love of God, and the faith which can keep men near His heart through time and eternity.

K. McA. P.

The Cure of Doing Something

Just before the Franco-Prussian war Von Moltke was in very poor health and had gone to Karlsbad for the cure. He was put on a careful diet, but his health bade fair to break down entirely. However, when news came of the declaration of war by France against Prussia, he brightened up and insisted upon going to the field. Within a few days he was well. He endured all the hardships of the service, often ate only bacon and bread, and kept his health until the war was over.

Such an incident may well be remembered when one reads remarkable tales of the cures wrought by this or that system of thought or teaching. We are sometimes asked how we "get around" such facts. No one has any business trying to "get around" any facts. They are always to be accepted when they are proved. But it is not always necessary to accept someone else's explanation of them. If a man tells you that he found a rabbit's foot one day and the next day began to prosper, you need not question either fact, but you may claim the privilege of doubting if they had anything to do with each other. If a man tells you that he read some hocus-pocus one day and the next day his rheumatism left him, you do not need to deny either of the facts, while you may feel free to find some other reason for the second than the mere occurrence of the first.

In many such incidents the fact is that a challenge to action came to the sufferer which turned his thought away from himself. Sometimes introducing and maintaining in the mind something stronger and more assertive than our bodily ills is all some of us need. If all women gave up as readily as some women do, homes would be mostly gone. If all men yielded to immediate feeling as some men do, business would end. It is because people do not quit, or because they see a good fight into which they can get, that many of them keep going.

No matter how much we differ about that physical principle, there is no doubt that some of the worse diseases of the soul are curable by doing something, by getting into the fight and forgetting spiritual ailments. When Elijah found the bottom dropped out of religion and the whole project of God, he needed first of all a long rest. Quiet, sleep, food—these were first, and God provided them. Still he was not ready to see the bright side of things. The first element of his cure was in God's sending him back to do something, to get into the fight again.

When Jesus asked Peter if he surely loved him, and Peter was certain that he did, Jesus did not tell him to be careful and watchful of his feelings. He told him to feed his sheep and to shepherd his lambs—that is, to do something, to get to work, to keep at work. That was the best way to keep his love alive.

Christ did not tell us that the people who "feel right" about him should "know of the doctrine whether it is from God or not." He swung the whole matter of assurance on obedience: "He that *doeth* the will shall know of the doctrine."

If you are in doubt about any vital thing of the faith, the first thing to do about it is to see that you are in the kind of fight that gives your soul a chance to be healthy. You are meant to be a warrior and the odds are immense that you will die if you stay on at a spiritual Karlsbad, but will grow lusty and strong if you will get into the battle somewhere. Get away from Karlsbad and get out where you are hard put to it. Find a place in the battle which God is waging. Try the cure of doing something.

The Boldness of Jesus

THERE is a familiar verse in the Acts which tells that when their enemies saw the boldness of Peter and John it surprised them into asking where they had been, and they seemed satisfied when they were told the two had been "with Jesus." The fact thus stated would seem better calculated to explain timidity and fear than boldness.

They had been with Jesus, but just where was Jesus at this time? So far as the official record went, he had been thoroughly and finally defeated. His project had failed. His disciples had been scattered. Of course there was some wild story about his having been raised from the dead, but there was a far more credible story told on official authority that the disciples had come by night while the guard slept and had carried away his body.

Put yourself in the place of any thoughtful man of the day and see if you feel that having been "with Jesus" would necessarily induce boldness. These disciples might well have been slinking off, ashamed.

Their boldness proved, for one thing, that they believed the story about his renewed life, and that took courage, just as it takes courage for a man today to stand up for the facts of the life of Christ.

But the deep, underlying reason for their boldness was that Jesus left an impression of unsurpassed boldness on all those who knew him. Their Master was bold, his disciples ought to be. Their Master was afraid of nothing. Never foolhardy, never risking life or favor needlessly, he yet held nobody in awe, short of God.

He said what he thought about anybody or anything. He went where he pleased and did what he pleased. He was well recognized as the deadliest foe there could be of the reigning religious hierarchy. He frankly warned his hearers against the hypocrites who were in power and who claimed special sanctity. He had not toadied to the rich for one instant; yet he had not toadied to the poor, either. He had told stories all over the country, some of which were against the rich and some against the poor. Even when the officials caught him, it had been in the easiest way possible. He had gone to a familiar place and they had gone at night and found him there. He had not been afraid. He had not tried to escape. He had not argued the case with the officers, and seemed even to scorn to defend himself before Pilate or Herod. He had gone to the cross without complaint. Nothing baffled him. If they knew anything about him, people knew that much. The disciples had a bold Master.

Neither his friends nor his foes in that day could perhaps have told why he was so fearless. We ought to know by now.

For one thing, he had the courage of the man who is attacking evil. It is always the men who stand aside who are afraid. Men in the thick of things have not time to be fearful. To them it is always worth while to do part of the task, if they cannot do it all. Jesus was always at it. So it always seemed feasible, at any rate always worth attempting.

His boldness came also from his complete trust in the methods he was using. They were slow methods, but they could not fail. Swords can fail; truths cannot. Spears can be blunted; ideas cannot. Power can be destroyed; love cannot. Self-assertion can go astray; self-sacrifice must win. Here was something that the world needed, and he was giving it to the world. That in itself was victory. The very loss of his life would be the saving of it. It was not necessary to see the success of his methods. They were bound to succeed. He knew life and the universe well enough for that.

But, of course, over and under everything else was the complete trust in his Father which made the whole way solid under his feet. His errand was not his alone; his Father was party to it. The battle was not his alone; it was God's battle. Nothing could finally defeat him, and what looked like defeat was sure to turn out a bit of victory in the end. In his days on earth Jesus may, or may not, have known just how a seeming defeat could be turned into victory, but his trust in his Father was unfailing and that insured the final outcome.

The matter that presses just now is whether his present disciples can be known for their having caught his boldness. Sometimes we hear remarks in meetings or even in pulpits that raise a question about it.

> *Now when they beheld the boldness of Peter and John, and had perceived that they were unlearned and ignorant men, they marvelled; and they took knowledge of them, that they had been with Jesus.*
>
> —Acts 4:13

The Important Things

How UTTERLY impossible it is to know at the time what are the important things!

Jesus' parable of the judgment, with its record of cups of cold water and visits to the sick, suggests how often things which were purely incidental and quickly forgotten are the things by which God judges.

Set in contrast with that the other declaration that there will come many at the last declaring they have preached and done wonderful things in his name, to whom Christ will say that he never knew them. That says nothing against those apparently greater things, for Jesus sent out his disciples to preach and to do great works of healing. But it does suggest how completely he keeps the matter of judgment in his own hands, and how little we know what are the important things.

We talk sometimes about "cardinal points" in life. The word *cardinal* comes from the Latin *cardo* which means a hinge, and cardinal points are those on which life hinges. We simply do not know when we come to one of those points.

Sometimes looking back we say that our whole life course was determined by some small act. Someone sneered at a proposal which was made, and that very fact turned us from it, and life has been different since then. The sneer was a cardinal point, though the man who sneered may have had no thought of the importance of it.

In his introduction to the life of Alexander, Plutarch defends his biographies by saying, "I do not write histories, but I write lives; and a slight circumstance, a jest, a word, is often a truer index to a man's character than accounts of his bloody victories and tremendous conquests." It is a familiar teaching that what a man does when he is off his guard is more revealing than his most prepared actions. The important word is not his formal declaration of his position, but often some chance clause in which he forgets himself, and so most fully asserts himself.

Everybody has a chance at God's big things. Nobody is kept back by the narrowness of his lot from doing the things which at the end will count most. The only danger in any lot is of a narrow spirit, an un-Christlike mind. Nobody knows what is chiefly important in any life. The only thing that is sure is that we shall be surprised when we find out.

All that seems left for us to do is to guard with equal care what we call small and great things, and to live by a spirit which will ennoble both.

Unbearable Troubles

Is THERE any such thing as an unbearable trouble? Carl Hilty says there is: "One can bear all troubles but two—worry and sin." Now it is well to realize that those two unbearable troubles are unnecessary. Neither worry nor sin has to be continued. Both can be ended by the large draft on the sovereign goodness of God which he is always ready to honor. As for other troubles, no one of them is unbearable. We are always surprised to see how much we can bear.

Most of us who seek to be wise would not look ahead ten years if we could. It would be impossible to bear the revelation of what will come to us in a decade. That would be putting the load of ten years on us in one day. In God's plan our experiences come to us gradually. Very few troubles come like lightning out of a clear sky. There are always clouds, and before the bolt falls there are flashes enough to prepare us somewhat for the shock. The cross is not laid upon our shoulders full weight at once. Rather, it comes down so slowly that those who must carry it can accommodate themselves to the load. God tempers the wind to the shorn lamb, but he sets out at once to protect the lamb, so that it can stand the next wind. A shorn lamb never stays shorn. The vital forces begin at once to prepare it for the cold of the next winter. It is in part this gradualness of God's dealing with us that makes trouble bearable.

Then there is much help in settling down quietly to the assurance that we are never to be broken by our troubles. There is no way of escaping them. It is not meant that we should be untroubled in this sense of the word. But it is assured that the wise hand that lets trouble come to us is also a strengthening hand that sustains us in trouble. When we are told to cast our burden upon the Lord, it is not said that he will take the burden away, but only that he will sustain us.

God is never taken unawares. If he is the only one who could foresee our troubles, then we have especial right to expect him to brace us to bear them. We could not be ready; therefore, he must help us, unready.

Most of us remember in driving through the country that a hill always looks steeper from across the valley than it proves to be when we come to its base and begin the ascent. Most of our troubles look far more serious to us ahead than they prove to be when we come to them. Sometimes we do not come to them at all; our road turns aside before we come to the steep hill. Sometimes we come to them just as we expected, but we always take them inch by inch, and we go our way through them in a strength which proves sufficient.

As our days our strength proves. We do not have strength for a decade today, but by the end of the decade a decade's strength has been doled out to us.

There is nothing to fear in the future. There is no water there deep enough to drown us, and no fire hot enough to burn us, and no burden heavy enough to crush us, because as we go into the future, Christ will be by us and bring us safely through. We could not bear the troubles alone, but he and we can bear them all.

The Consecration of a Sorrow

THE MOST puzzling question which comes to Christian people at a time of great sorrow is, Why?

There is little use in telling us that we ought not to ask it. It is true that we may not be able to find a full answer, yet there is more answer than most of us find, for most of us look in the wrong place. We look back to find what precedes our experience to learn the reason which God had for letting us have it. The best reasons for God's greatest deeds, as far as we know them, lie after the deeds themselves. Most of us will find the best answer by looking forward.

It is not so much what has preceded the sorrow as what shall follow it; not what the sorrow follows, but what follows the sorrow. In the case of the greatest sorrow the world has ever known the reason for it followed it. There is no adequate explanation for the death of Christ in any of the events which preceded it. The redemption of the world which is steadily following it is the only adequate explanation.

When we find ourselves maimed and broken, we get no comfort in looking back and seeing that it was our fault and that it might have been different if we had done this or that. Constant brooding on the irrevocable is useless. Here is the experience, whatever was the cause of it. No matter if we see a thousand things that might have changed this, it cannot now be changed. Very well, then, what shall we do with it in the days that are coming? Since we cannot see God's reasons behind us, let us work his reasons out in the days that are before us. What made the sorrow is not half as important as what the sorrow can make of us.

You have lost your little child, and you are completely staggered by it. Friends suggest to you banal or even wicked reasons why God allowed this sorrow to come on you. The reason may not lie behind you at all but altogether before you. It may lie in the future of your child. It may lie in the future of your own heart. It is absolutely sure that God means the sorrow to do a great thing for you. If you let it shut you in from the world so that you grow indifferent to the world's great sorrow, you have done the loving Father an injustice. That sorrow opened a path straight from your feet out to the needy world. You know better now what loads are, and what disappointments are, and what failure is. For one reason and another the world is full of all these things. You are one of God's marked men hereafter, for you have passed through an experience that has in it the making of might.

Keep your eyes forward. Don't look back to find the reason why God let your sorrow come to you. Be very sure his richest reason lies in what he and you together can make of it in the days and years ahead.

A Plea for the Common in Us All

EVERYBODY is somewhat peculiar; if in nothing else at least in the fact that he is himself and not another person. We often say that no two leaves are alike, and it is equally commonplace to say that no two persons are ever alike. Twins are sometimes described as being so alike that their own mother cannot tell them apart, but it is only in extravagant humor that we pretend that the twins do not know each other apart. Each is just himself, and is never really confused with the other.

Actually the only thing that gives value to our own peculiarities is that most people don't have them, and in that particular at least we are uncommon. If all of us were exactly alike, no one of us could do anything striking.

Marshall Field came from a little town in Massachusetts and developed a great store in Chicago, but if everybody in Chicago had developed a great department store, then Marshall Field could not have done it. It was the commonness of other people at the point of his peculiarity that gave him his chance. We say that Abraham Lincoln was a man of the common people. So he was. But he must have been something else. Why did not a thousand men of the common people do what he did? Manifestly, it was the uncommonness in him that determined his service. Yet it is equally manifest that the commonness of other people brought him into such bold relief that his peculiar power found its opportunity. A republic in which everybody is president, a war in which everybody is commander in chief, a reform in which everybody is the leader, is as unthinkable as one in which there is no president or commander or leader.

The point to be made is this: If other people have to be common in order that we may be peculiar, or that our special powers may have their best play, why should we not learn to be content to be common at some points so that other men can be uncommon? Why should we allow any tinge of jealousy to creep over our estimate of other people? All of us are needed. Suppose the workaday things chafe us. Suppose there are some people who seem to get out of them. Most people cannot. The Ecclesiastes writer puts the matter keenly in his familiar saying: "The king himself is served by the field." Let the work of the field cease and the king will suffer. If we are jealous of the king, it must be because we want someone else to do work we think is beneath us to do.

We must all take our share of the commonplace. A diplomat was surprised to find Lincoln polishing his shoes. He exclaimed, "Do you polish your own shoes?" "Yes," Lincoln answered. "Whose shoes do you polish?"

If it is not shoes, it must be something else. Most people must be common at most points in order that all may be uncommon at some points.

Little Evils Go with Big Ones

IT SEEMS difficult for some men to realize that you cannot have a big wrong without a whole series of details which issue from it. They get their minds fixed on the details and bemoan them without seeing that they are perfectly natural.

Take, for example, our feeling about the outrages practiced in the course of a war. What else did we expect? Dropping bombs, laying mines, outraging villages, shelling churches and hospitals—of course. They may all be expected when war comes. Complaint of them is much like complaining that the murderer, when he came in to commit murder, muddied the carpet and broke a Sevres vase. Of course he did. Conceivably he might have stopped to paint a portrait or play a sonata while he waited for his victim to die, but generally a man in the mood for murder is in the mood for any incidental damage that goes along with it.

War is elementally a brutal thing and brutal incidents are part of it. Negotiations to moderate the violence of war practices when no war is on are commendable, but most of them fly to the winds when the war actually comes. A group of men come together saying, "We do not expect to kill each other, of course, but let us agree that if later we do decide to kill, we will not stick a knife into each other under the fourth rib, but always under the fifth; and we will not break the watch crystal in the victim's pocket nor dent his derby hat." And then, when the killing begins, they center their horror on the terrible facts that

46

the watch crystal was broken and the hat was dented in and, worst of all, the knife was actually under the fourth rib!

Outrages? Of course. Did we think war was a series of afternoon teas? Did we suppose an army was a group of well-trained nursemaids out for an airing? The business of war is essentially damaging. It intends to put men out of service; it plans to destroy the power of men and if necessary to destroy the men themselves. Is it to be expected that men who consider it necessary to their purpose to do these things will balk at details which add shades of horror to the scene?

It is all a piece with the constant effort of the human race to cure evil by bits, to stop a bad habit here and a wrong custom there.

The proposal of our Christian faith is a new heart, a new center of living power, a blow at the sinfulness which is at the root of great wrongs. When the big evils are corrected, the little evils are taken care of.

So Great a Salvation

CHRISTIANITY is nothing if not an offer and an achievement of salvation from sin. No period has ever been without schemes for reducing it to a system of ethics, or a fine bit of example, or to a code of truths. The schemes have their day and disappear, to be succeeded by more schemes. Each has its value. The weakness of each is that it misses the central purpose of Christianity and substitutes for it some wholly subsidiary purpose.

The Founder and Object of the Christian faith received his name not from the fact that he would teach his people many important truths, though he does that; not from the fact that he would show them how to live better lives, though he steadily does that; not from the fact that he would lay out for them a program of advancement in grace and power and wisdom, though he surely does that; but from the fact that he would save his people from their sins. It is for this that his name is called Jesus.

All these other services enter into any complete work of saving ministry, but neither singly nor all taken together do they reveal the greatness of the salvation which changes and cleanses the hearts and lives of sinful men.

The fundamental presumption of the Christian faith is that men are sinful—not that they are essentially good and only incidentally bad. Confucianism insists that all men are born good. They are like streams of pure water issuing from a spring. The stream will doubtless become defiled with the dirt through which it passes as it runs down the hillside, but all that is needed is to let it settle and the dirt will disappear, leaving the water clear again.

Christianity does not start with that presumption. It is not dealing with a weak world primarily, which merely needs strengthening; not with an ignorant world which needs teaching; not with a poor world which needs enriching; but with a sinful world which needs saving, a wrong world which needs righting, an offending world which needs atonement. All the weakened forms of the Christian faith cheapen the idea of salvation by clouding the idea of sinfulness.

If Confucianism is right, then all that the human soul needs is a chance—some influence or condition which will give its natural powers a way to develop. If Christianity is right, then the human soul needs a change—some work done in it which will alter what has come to be its governing principle.

Doubtless this seems an unattractive proposition for the church to preach. Most congregations would naturally rather have it said that they are all essentially good; that the old doctrine of evil natures is abandoned by all thinking men; that all any man needs to be a good man is to quit his meanness and just be good; that the only reason any man does wrong is because he is not careful to think before he acts, and that therefore salvation consists in being different ourselves.

George Eliot once suggested that everybody has his own favorite "opium" which he takes whenever he comes into presence of a trying thing. We have just been talking about sayings and opinions which are the opium of many souls, which they take when they face the fact of their own tendencies and the obvious drift of life. They would like to think they could get on without the strong sanctions of religion and the regenerating grace of Almighty God. But that theory has come tumbling down about our very ears. Something bigger and stronger than human plans can provide must be brought into the human situation or we are in a parlous state. It is just this bigger, stronger thing that the Christian faith provides: not a chance for the human heart, but a change.

When one does face the facts of life without "opium" the proposal of the Christian faith to take account primarily of the root fact of sin is most attractive. The salvation which is offered looms large beside all other proposals. The subsidiary services of teaching the ignorant and strengthening the weak and enriching the impoverished world are left in their proper and important places. No faith renders these services so well as the Christian faith. But the great salvation it provides is from age-long, ruinous, deep-rooted sin.

Removable Limitations

THERE are no unlimited men. Nobody can do everything. Nobody has so much money or so much time or so many powers that he is never stopped when he would like to go forward. The richest men cannot keep their sons from death by disease. The most eloquent men cannot always rise to their full power, and they cannot be eloquent about everything. The bravest leaders cannot go forward faster or farther than their followers will follow. Each man is in a circle which limits him, and most of his limitations are out of his own power or reach.

But not all limitations are out of everybody's power. Many are removable. Some men cannot do their best because other men limit them where they ought not to be limited. They are like Lazarus just out of the grave; the grave clothes were put on him by others, not by himself, and it was only fair that they take them off again. He had ample power to walk or run so far as he was concerned, but the limitations which others had put on him without his consent must be taken away. Many a man stands tied and limited by bonds which others have imposed on him, and which these others must remove before he has his real chance. It is of a piece with the great broad fact that we are all our brother's keepers. Men are so bound in the one bundle of life that each is dependent on the others.

If a limitation is removable, wise men will work to remove it.

When God's Clock Strikes

SOME of us can remember when we were told the story of the plan of Abraham for the sacrifice of Isaac. We watched the departure of the father and son from the home; we watched them make their journey to the mountain; we watched them go up to the mountaintop; we heard Isaac ask his father where they were to find the sacrifice for the wood which they were carrying. The condition grew more tense as we went on. We saw the altar built, and the wondering Isaac bound and laid on it. Then we saw Abraham's hand raise the knife to offer the sacrifice.

It all comes back as we go over the story again. What if God had not spoken just then? What if Abraham had not heard that voice and turned and looked and found the ram caught in the thicket?

Our wise mothers, having brought us to the climax, always made us feel that God is never too late, that he always comes when we have to have him and that he never missed the connection with our life's need. Doctors come too late; fathers and mothers arrive when the trouble is over; but God never comes too late. The great things never happen until God's time comes.

When God's clock strikes, then things may happen. When they do occur, therefore, we have a right to say that his clock had struck. Can we miss the comfort and assurance of that? We are such busy, bustling people, and we strain so to bring things to pass, and are so distressed when there are any delays. Or we are so concerned when things happen prematurely, according to our judgment. Can we not learn to lie quietly down upon the assurance that God has his hour when his great events occur? Somewhere around our free agency his mold clamps down and the great events come in their time.

The realization ought to give us a great feeling of safety. It does not take away from us the possibility of doing unwise and rash things. It leaves us much to repent of. But after all, it suggests that there are Hands over ours which really control the matters that count.

We sometimes wonder why we do not do things, and we make labored explanations of our human delays. Then there comes to us a revealing lightning flash, which shows that we are working under a plan. That plan never encourages one of us in indolence or idleness. It brings us constant inspiration that the purposes which God has are sure to be brought out, and that we are to put ourselves in line with them.

The victory is not under discussion; it is assured. When the hour strikes for it, it will come.

But on which side we shall be when it comes—ah! that is for us to say.

(The story of Abraham and Isaac is in the 22nd chapter of Genesis, verses 1-14.)

Three Stages of Thankfulness

Being thankful is something. It is more than some of us are equal to. A man has a valuable ability when he can overlook certain disquieting experiences in the interest of undisturbed causes for gratitude.

What a blessed thing it is that we are able to forget so much! It is probable that you could not name offhand ten events in the year that was ten years ago. There were days that went hard with you; there were weeks that dragged and seemed almost to kill you; there were events which seemed to you so tangled that you could not get away from them. Perhaps they made it difficult for you to be thankful. Yet here you are and you have forgotten most of them. Be sure that is the attitude which ten years from now you will take toward this year. Many of the things which make the feeling of thankfulness difficult will drop out of your thinking, and in a decade they will not disturb you. Why not then manage to overlook them now in the interest of larger and undisturbed blessings for which you can be unqualifiedly thankful? *Being thankful* is something, and it is always possible.

Giving thanks is more. "Let the redeemed of the Lord say so," one of the writers says. Keeping thanks bottled up within one is certain to sour them. The only way to keep any vital thing sweet is to keep it moving. To be thankful and to make no manifestation of it is either a contradiction in terms or will soon result in the loss of the spirit of thankfulness.

In the Hebrews it is urged that we "offer up a sacrifice of

praise to God continually; that is, the fruit of lips which make confession to his name." It does not do to take the knowledge of our thankfulness too much for granted. Jesus expressed his own feeling regarding the nine who, though they were cured, did not return to express their gratitude. There are husbands who take it for granted that their wives know their love for them, and many a domestic unhappiness has come from the fact that husbands have not said the things which they feel ought to be taken for granted. For our own sakes, as well as for the sake of God, we must give thanks as well as feel thankful.

Making thankful is more still. Being thankful may have in it a spirit of selfishness, giving thanks may develop a spirit of pride, but making thankful, enriching someone else's life, is sure to save one from selfishness and pride.

Thanksgiving Day, as every day, is better for seeing to it that someone else is thankful. It was the principle involved in the old regime, when Nehemiah commanded that portions should be sent to those who were without. It is this that deepens and strengthens our own spirit of thanksgiving.

God's Will Is Not Second Best

WHAT do we Christians think about God's will? Judging by ordinary expressions about it, we think it is the next best thing to our own will. When it crosses ours, we speak regretfully about it. We cannot have our own way; therefore "The Lord's will be done." We even feel virtuous that we do not rebel. We praise each other for accepting God's will so sweetly.

Surely we ought to have an exultant feeling when we have found God's will. What a marvel it is that he should have any will for us! Who are we that he should have any plan covering our lives? Why should we not be allowed to go on our own foolish way, that way which we so much prefer, without any concern of his? The very fact that his will differs from ours is proof that our will was a long second best, and we have been mercifully kept from it. We cannot prefer it once we know what his will is. We do not submit to his will; we spring to it. We release our own because we are sure it was not a good will.

There is a tombstone on a child's grave in England which has this inscription:

> A gardener was going round the garden with his master and came upon a young and tender flower plucked off. He asked, "Who plucked this flower?" "I did," replied the master. And the gardener held his peace.

Yes, but the gardener did not hold his peace because he felt that he was compelled to submit to his master's will. He was raising that flower for his master and his own will was fulfilled in the will of his master.

This is easier to talk about in cold blood than to feel in the hot blood of sorrow, but it is the spirit that belongs to believers. God's will is not second best. It is uniformly and always best, and when it crosses ours it is still evidence of his own goodness.

Secretary John Hay wrote a great hymn in which he points out that Christian believers are not called on to accept God's will in dumb resignation, or like nerveless fatalists, but that their faith is meant to soar like the eagle and to cry exulting, "O Lord, thy will be done!"

We so easily lose this attitude toward God's will. Our minds run so readily to submission. Instead, they need to run to joyous inspiration because of the existence of a will so great that it can command us, and that loves us enough to cross us if that is best.

Being Loyal to the Future

WE ARE forever hearing talk about being loyal to the past. We must keep the faith once committed to the saints. We must be worthy of our ancestry.

Quite as sound a word can be said about loyalty to the future. Our ancestors are not really so important as our posterity. The saints to whom the faith was delivered are not all behind us; some are yet to be born.

We do not honor our faith by wrapping it in a napkin and passing it on exactly as we found it. The trust committed to us by our fathers in our faith is a living one. We must hand it on to our children enriched, developed, enlarged. It is to go back into the hand of the Master not as we received it but representing our own toil and enterprise.

Sometimes church officers grow so proud of their history, and so sure of the blessing of God upon plans already tried, and so loyal to the past, that they leave out of account their responsibility to the future. They have no right to lay such narrow plans that they will cramp their children. They have no right to be so fearful that they will not attempt tasks which would be worthy for their sons to take up.

For one thing, the future is greater than the past. There is more to be done than has been done. It is part of the weakness of us all that we have too small ideas of the plans of God for the future. We take petty views of what is yet to be and we cannot realize that the past is the smallest part of history. It is not evening twilight in which we are walking; it is morning twilight. God's day is just getting started. We have no right to treat the past as though it were the greatest of God's periods of time.

For another thing, the future has more claims on us than the past has. It has more interests trembling in the balance. The past, to be sure, does depend upon us partly to justify it and partly to confirm it. We sometimes say, "The past at least is secure," but as a matter of fact a great deal of it is not secure until we make it so. Our fathers handed down to us a great many unfinished plans. The part they did is not approved until we have done our part.

And yet the past is far more secure than the future. We will set forward or greatly handicap the next generation by the way we take life. Solomon builds a more magnificent temple because David prepares the materials for him. As David looks at his life, he owes something to Jesse, his father, but he owes more to Solomon, his son.

Then also, the future depends on us as the past does not. We are steadily bringing the future into being. We are shaping its course for it. We are more and more setting the mold into which it must be poured. It will be harder and harder for those who come after us to break away from what we have been and have done.

Loyalty to the future is the great demand. The real question about plans, or faith, or life, is not: Do they honor the past? But: Are they what will insure the future?

Honest Questions

IN THE religious life there are just three types of questions. Some are idle, some are dishonest, some are honest. The real test is whether we mean to shape our lives by the answer when we get it; whether we are ready to obey the truth if we should find it.

There are many purely idle questions. The answer would make no sort of difference to us if we got it. We do not ask it because we really want to know, but because we are curious about some indifferent matter. It is of interest to know where Cain got his wife, and what was Paul's thorn in the flesh. The questions are worth asking as matters of interest, but so far as the Christian life is concerned they are, of course, idle questions. No matter how they are answered, duty is exactly the same.

So with questions that are simply dishonest, where we pretend to be concerned and are not. We ask if the Bible is inspired, and we have already settled that it is, or is not, so far as we are concerned. We do not mean to obey the answer if we get it. It is only a nominal question. We have not come with an honest and open mind to it.

But there are honest questions. There is simply no avoiding them in living our normal lives. There are things that it seems to us we must know.

Of course, questions which are idle to some become vital to others. Take the matter of miracles. There are some people who are not at all troubled about them. There are others to whom they are vital. Or the matter of the Trinity, or the deity of our

Lord. It is easy enough for some people to accept these great truths and raise no question about them. Others find themselves persistently faced by grave problems connected with them. Their questions are absolutely honest. They want to live by the truth which they discover. They mean to shape their lives by it when they find it. What is to be said about these questions?

For one thing, it must be frankly recognized that there are some questions whose answer does not readily come to any of us. There is in the whole Christian life an element of faith. We simply do not know, for example, how to answer the question why God deals with us as he does, except in the broad assurance of fatherly love. We believe that his ways are all wise and kindly and best. But neither the wisdom, nor the kindness, nor the goodness always appears to us. We must take them by faith. We can probably never come to an entirely satisfactory explanation of the fact of the Trinity, nor of the way by which Christ could be God and man. We are dealing with infinite matters and cannot hope for a finite explanation.

But the facts are not unsettled because the questions are not answered. We do not know the explanation of the facts, but we know the facts. How to explain the Trinity is one thing, but the Trinity is quite another. Jesus did not tell Nicodemus "how these things could be" but contented himself simply with reasserting them. We do not yet know the answer to Nicodemus' question except in the form of an assertion. The explanation is not given, but the fact abides.

(The story of Nicodemus' visit to Jesus "by night" is told in the third chapter of John, verses 1-16.)

Public Goodness

NOTHING in the Bible forbids public goodness. It is not said that we are not to do our alms before men. The fact is, it is often a good thing to let goodness be seen. It is our way of letting our light shine before men. It acquaints some people with the appearance of righteousness which they might never see otherwise. They have to see it in other people or not see it at all.

There can be a humility in churches which is hurtful. There can be a hiding which is a hindering. Many a church is made more enthusiastic and earnest by hearing of the good work that is being done elsewhere and of the blessing that is coming there.

A congregation can often be stirred into a cash consideration of foreign missions more quickly by a symposium of news of the work actually being done than by reading the last chapter of Matthew or the first chapter of Romans. One is goodness that is quiet and lowers its voice. The other is goodness that is making a stir and talking in italics in order to start more goodness going.

We lay stress on the quietness of Jesus' life and work, speaking of how he put the crowd out when he was about to work a miracle; and how he told a man not to tell what he had done; and how he wanted no man to know that he was in a certain place. All that is true. Yet we are specially told of the time when he went into the temple and cried with a loud voice in the midst of the crowd, drawing the eyes of all men to himself and their ears to his message. He told one man to go back and tell all his friends what great things the Lord had done for him. He told his disciples to go everywhere telling about him and his work.

Jesus did not love publicity, but he did not fear it. He would not let them make him a king, but he told Pilate the reason why. He was already a king and did not need human crowning or laurel. He bids us proclaim everywhere his salvation, yet his salvation is simply himself. God has printed his name and his power everywhere. You cannot look at a mountain or a mite without having a chance to see or hear God.

No, public goodness is not forbidden. The thing that is rebuked is goodness that is good only for the sake of publicity. It is righteousness that wants to be looked at before it cares to be right. It is kindness that would be cruel if it were behind the scenes. There is enough "goodness" of that kind to explain why we are all shy about praising it when it does become public. But men who are unwilling to let God's goodness to them, and through them, be known are not necessarily so very humble. They may in fact be thinking of themselves, afraid of what men may say about them, but not thinking enough about what men may be led to say about their Lord.

Has any follower of Christ a right to hide his goodness and let men suppose he is selfish and stingy when actually he is helping broadly and generously? How then are men to know what the grace of God has done in his life?

No man is to let his light shine that men may see *him;* but every man is to let his light shine that other men may glorify the Father in heaven.

"Go, Tell His Disciples"

THE EASTER news was amazing news. Those who needed to hear it first were the disciples. It was they whose hopes had been dashed into helplessness. It was they to whom it made the whole world of difference that Jesus had risen from the grave and conquered death. "His disciples" will always understand the meaning of the resurrection. The rabble in Jerusalem will give explanations of it that destroy the fact. Learned chief priests would rather concoct a story out of pure imagination than accept the fact that Jesus rose from the dead. If history is not as they wish it, they will create history. It is disciples who understand.

Remember that the disciples had not expected the resurrection. It seemed to them that the chapter was closed, closed as a tragedy. Their talk on the way to Emmaus fell naturally into the past tense: "We hoped that it was he who should redeem Israel." Hope was gone by this time. Their faith could not make the fact of their Master's resurrection, but their love was enough to make them understand the fact when they knew it. Their past experience with Jesus was so rich that it was ready to be brought to fruitage under a genial sun.

Such a sun rose in the wholly unexpected fact of Christ still living. Under its shining, seeds of experience grew and expanded. What they had not understood before began to grow clear. Occasionally we read that the disciples understood this and that saying only after his resurrection. Any man who ever walked through a room in the dark and then had the light turned on will know what that means. The disciples had been walking through the dark with him. The resurrection cleared up many mysteries.

It has been so with his later followers. We can understand many things in the light of the resurrection which are merely baffling without it. If the cross ends things, then we have only one more illustration of the fact that goodness is a failure in this world. But if the cross ends nothing, and only opens the way to larger things, it will reassure us that goodness is so mighty that it can triumph over death itself.

Personal sorrows show their transitory face in presence of it. The loss of loved ones becomes an unmeasured gain as they are seen passing, not into the grave but through it. Until the resurrection grows clear to the vision, all footprints lead toward the tomb. In its light are seen footprints leading away from its farther side. Only discipleship sees them clearly. Men who do not hear as disciples doubt the news or deny it, or fail to catch its meaning. When the disciples hear it, experiences flock to it, finding their confirmation in it.

Let no one wonder, then, that men with the skeptical heart underread the great story. Its meaning is too vast for any heart which has not been opened to the love of the Father, and given in loyal discipleship to his Son.

Listening to the Invisible

MOSES is the central figure in a painting of law-givers which George Frederick Watts painted on a wide wall of Lincoln's Inn where attorneys and lawyers congregate. Mohammed, Alfred, Charlemagne and Justinian stand out from the others, but Moses is head and shoulders above them all, and he alone has the uplifted head and face, as though listening to something higher than human argument. It is a painter's recognition of the pre-eminence of Moses among lawgivers and of the real source of his inspiration. He listened to the Invisible. The law that came to him came not up from the soil of Egypt or the desert, nor from the granite of Sinai. He saw it in all these fields of life, but he knew its source to be above them all. It came to him out of the Invisible.

We have so many laws now that we are apt to forget that there is law. We see so plainly how our laws came to be that we grow blind to that law which never came to be from any human source but is written in the nature of things by the finger of God. There will always be case-triers who will twist and warp human laws in the interest of clients who want their way and have no zeal for righteousness. But we shall always have for our great lawyers men who can hear the Invisible and know that the Voice heard there will soon or late drown out the conflicting voices of legislatures.

We all need the same hint for our lives. Ministers are in constant peril of yielding to the rush and bustle of life which makes them deaf to the Invisible. The clatter of a church office takes the place of the quiet of a minister's study. A city pastor bemoaned recently that he was virtually never out of the hearing of a typewriter and a telephone. Some clergymen accept all this as inevitable and even as desirable. Ministers must be "men, first of all," they insist. They must show businessmen that they are men of affairs and can run an office as well as the best of them; so they pride themselves on the up-to-date methods which obtain in their "studies."

We are fairly familiar with the argument and we know the force of it, but we are not convinced. Is the hearing of our ministers today so much clearer than their fathers' that they can hear that august Voice without the quiet of the soul in which the fathers heard it? Granted that we have not enough church "office," is it not certain that we have too little minister's "study"? We beg our ministers, as they hope to stand before their fellows speaking for God, that they find time and place for listening to the Invisible, for meditation, for prayer, for quiet thinking and hard study, giving God a chance at their souls.

We dare to make a similar plea to all burdened ones. There are many books of comfort in sorrow and distress. Those that help us to hear the voice of God are the best ones. Counsel to drown our troubles in work, to forget, to divert our minds may help some of us sometimes. Our real help comes when we turn our ears toward the Invisible. Books, unless it be the Book, are only channels through which the stream of help comes from the true fountain. Let us learn the way to the fountain for ourselves. Let us listen to the Invisible, lifting our sorrow and trouble up with us and finding them made endurable by the Voice that comes from the heights.

Anywhere, Only Forward!

DAVID LIVINGSTONE had been sent by the London Missionary Society to the Bechuanas, but the field was too small for the force at hand and he set out for another place, hoping for the approval of the directors of the society but telling them that he was at their disposal "to go anywhere, *provided it be forward.*" One of his natural traits was to go forward. The venerable Dr. Isaac Taylor of Ongar, who knew David Livingstone in youth, said, "Now, after nearly forty years, I remember his step, the characteristic forward tread, firm, simple, resolute, neither fast nor slow, no hurry and no dawdle, but which evidently meant *getting there.*" The characteristic forward tread!

The largest distress in life for thoughtful men is to be shut in from any advance. In Dickens' *Hard Times* he makes one of his characters declare that life is only a muddle: the town is rich; there are numbers of people who are brought there to weave and to card and to piece out a living; the mills are always going; yet the workers never come nearer to any distant object, except always death. The town has grown, but life has not grown, and though men are laboring hard, they are not getting anywhere. They are stepping, but not forward. They are going at breakneck speed, but they are not going anywhere.

The question to put about any plan or any work is: *Does it get anywhere?* Is it just a round that does not fit into any plan of progress? The real question is not about the size of the task. Even a small task, if it is fitting into an ongoing plan, is worthier than a larger task which does nothing after all. Your church, for example. Is it going backward? Is it holding its own? Or is it going forward? Are your methods with it, your policies in it, your plans for it, getting it forward at all? Or have you settled down to the feeling that just holding your own is enough?

You are a layman, let us say. What is your attitude toward proposals for work? Are you eager for them? Or are you always tired and afraid to see any big things attempted? There are men who are content to work in the Bechuana field even if it is well manned. They would let well enough alone. There is tremendous need for men who have a characteristic forward tread, who are willing to set out on anything providing it leads forward, and who cannot stay in conditions which do not lead out into larger and worthier fields.

Getting the Second Wind

PROFESSOR WILLIAM JAMES first put into words the interesting fact, which many of us have experienced, that in great physical effort there is a very early stage when one seems exhausted and unable to go on. If then, by sheer force of will, one does go on, there comes a re-enforcement of strength, the weariness and exhaustion pass away, and the following period of endurance is longer than the first one.

Professor James suggests that there may be reserves of strength, reservoirs of physical power, which we tap from time to time as we go on. A runner knows that very well. Anyone who watches by a sickbed realizes how the early part of the night is often more exhausting than the latter part. We have our second wind.

What is true on a physical basis is good for all parts of life and work. There is a first flush of strength and success, when everything is promising, and then there comes an exhaustion which is often a time of great despair. If then, by dogged and determined effort of will, and by a sense of God's desire, a man will hold himself to his work, ceasing to look elsewhere or think elsewhere, he may have full faith in a new reservoir of strength which he will tap, whose current will be stronger and whose water will be more refreshing than that which he first found.

Businessmen know about it. Young fellows who have taken positions and have been so sure that they have found just their place have also in a few months been ready to accept something else. If they had waited to catch their breath again they would have found themselves ready to go on for years, to larger success.

For that matter, this is a common experience in the Christian life itself. The losses after revival meetings are outstanding illustrations of it. Many of these converts were runners who struck a rapid pace at the first and did not know enough to keep moving when their breath seemed gone, in the assurance that there was a second wind awaiting them for the long run.

Most of us have had experiences which made us think we would have to give up the Christian life. We were dismal failures in it and might as well end it first as last. Then appeared some friend, or some family training asserted itself, and we held on, more as a matter of form than anything else. It did not seem quite decent to give up just then. So we pegged away at our Christian duty. Presently our second wind came. We tapped a new reservoir of strength, and we have gone on ever since.

When a man is sure he is in the way God wants him to go, he can afford to keep going, perfectly sure that at every point in the road God has new supplies awaiting him.

Praying with Open Eyes

IT IS a wise and helpful custom to close the eyes in prayer. The world intrudes on us so persistently that when we want to realize God's presence we must shut out its diverting, confusing sights. So it is a wise custom to have places of solitude for prayer, where the sounds as well as the sights of the world can be shut out. He is a strange son of the Father who does not know the meaning of being shut in alone with him.

But the soul has its eyes and they are to be open at their widest when we pray. They see God and they see the world also.

The late Bishop Whipple of Minnesota told of one of his clergy who was called to comfort a dying girl. The house in which she lay was "kept by an incarnate devil" who was much offended that he should pray there. Still, he went several times on his errand of mercy. Finally the woman met him with a knife, saying that he was not to pray in that house again. He had in his hand a stout walking stick and turned to her and said very courteously, "Madam, I came here to commend this dying girl to Jesus Christ. I can pray with my eyes open. I shall now pray, and if you stir one step while I am praying I will break your head with this stick." So he prayed.

In far less literal sense our Lord has commended the same plan in bidding us *watch* and *pray*. There are some to whom watching is easier than praying, and some to whom praying is easier than watching, but the strongest prayers we offer are those in which our eyes are open to the facts and the needs regarding which we pray. Going into the closet and closing the door is not meant to keep us from seeing the world, but to keep the world from seeing us.

The habit of praying with the eyes of the soul wide open will meet the objection which young Christians raise, that they do not know what to pray for. Let anyone open his eyes to his own needs and the needs of the world about him and he will find plenty to lay before God for his help. Could anyone live in a city with its problems, or in the country with its needs, and know them, see them with open eyes, and then, finding himself alone with God, have no prayer to offer?

Gilbert Chesterton points to a familiar difference between two types of sainthood. The Buddhist saint is always represented with a sleek, comfortable body, and with closed eyes, lost in meditation. The Christian saint may be wasted to a mere skeleton, but he is always painted with his eyes wide open, looking bravely at the world. It is a valid distinction. The Christian faith does not shut our eyes, save that we may see more clearly. We pray, but we watch also, and our watching makes our praying more eager.

The Humble Heart

"THE MEEK shall inherit the earth." Yes, say the scornful from their seats, the meek shall inherit just enough earth to be buried in. It is the strong, the assertive who get the earth. All of us share the feeling in part. It appears in the constant protest we make against representing Christ as anemic or effeminate. Make him appear virile, we say. Hear his voice pronouncing the woes on the hypocrites. Remember how men fell back from him in the garden and slunk away from him when he challenged them to cast a stone if they were without sin. This is the Christ we need.

Doubtless the church does need a large accent on his manly bearing and strong character. Yet we shall lose immensely if we gain this conception of strength by any surrender of the meekness of our Lord. Bluster and hard-handedness are no substitutes for gentleness. Self-assertion will not take the place of meekness. The humble heart is still the dwelling place of the Lord of the universe. The meek do inherit the earth. It is Christ's gentleness that has made him great. He is not to be found in his conquering power on battlefields, however his presence is there invoked. His victories will not be won by weapons of destruction. Instead, in our hospitals, our refuges for the distressed, our quiet homes, our business offices where honesty rules and brotherliness controls, our agencies for the help of the weak, the needy, the broken—there we find Christ in his really regnant power.

Actually no great conquest of life is by bluster. Only cheap victories come out of mere noise and clamor and self-assertion. It is an old word of Bacon: "The kingdom of learning, like the kingdom of heaven, can be entered only by the spirit of a little child." And Huxley's word ought to be familiar: "Science seems to me to teach in the highest and strongest manner the great truth which is embodied in the Christian conception of entire surrender to the will of God. Sit down before fact as a little child, be prepared to give up every pre-conceived notion, follow humbly wherever and to whatever abyss nature leads, or you shall learn nothing. I have only begun to learn content and peace of mind since I resolved at all risk to do this." That is high testimony to the need of the humble heart in science.

Only the humble heart prepares us to learn God's will for our lives. Not until we have come to the point of choosing his will without knowing what that will is have we come to the point of finding that will. We are called always to walk in the dark in the beginning of obedience. If we must wait to find his will before we choose it, we are not choosing his will but our own which chances to agree. The soldier who must have his marching orders fully stated before he enlists is not agreeing to follow his commander's lead. He is agreeing only to what commends itself to him.

Washington complained that his soldiers could be trusted only when there was time to explain the commands to them, and he hoped the time would come (as it did) when they would trust their commander's reasons because the commands came from him. When someone chided Mr. Lincoln that the army was making little progress, he replied that the men were just now learning to obey. Until then, each man had his own plan of campaign which he thought was better than his commander's plan.

So it goes with us. Until our hearts are humble, we cannot find God's will.

Only the humble heart can do God's will consciously. We can do the things for which his will calls while our heads are high and our necks are stiff. Pharaoh did the things for which God's will called. So did Napoleon, we may suppose. Yet neither did God's will in itself. The heart of neither was with the will of God. The heart of each was with his own will. Men may preach the gospel, serve in church offices, go as missionaries, only doing the things which God's will calls for, and yet not be doing his will.

The distinction is important. Choosing the will of God and taking the things it demands as incidental is one thing; choosing the things which accord with his will but with no purpose of doing his will is a vastly different thing. Only the humble heart keeps itself so out of the way that God's will itself gets right of way.

Only the humble heart can do God's will joyously. The heavy heart, the dreary heart, may be found toiling on in the way of his will, accepting it even when it clashes with the heart's own desires, but finding no joy in the service. The joy of obedience waits for the meek spirit. "Content and peace of mind" have come to more than Huxley when men have determined to sit humbly before God and let him choose the way. That way becomes a joyous one to the humble heart. Pride or self-assertion makes that way hard and steep. The meek and heavy-laden find the yoke easy and the burden light.

"Guard Me in My Strength"

WE CAN generally be trusted with our weaknesses. We know where they are and what they are. We are on the lookout in their behalf. Our strength is more deceptive. One of the early saints prayed: "Guard me in my strength; I fall by it more sadly than by my weaknesses."

Churches often pride themselves on their striking traits. We see other churches pushing their work aggressively by noisy methods, and we thank God that "our church does not run on brass band lines." Or we see other churches moving along in their sedate ways, doing everything slowly and conservatively, and we thank God that "our church is alive and not a walking corpse." Others may receive new members by the score; we are glad that "our church is not a mere mob." Or else others may be receiving only a few; we are glad that "our church is no mere fashionable club for the elect." So it goes, each church tending to show the weakness of its strength, and each one needing some measure of the very thing it dislikes in the others.

It will not hurt any of us to pray as the early saint prayed: "Guard me in my strength; I fall by it more sadly than by my weaknesses."

How Do You Measure God's Love?

THE STORY is going around of a little girl who burst in upon her mother with the cry that God did not love her any more. The mother reassured her that God always loves everybody. But the child wailed, "No, Mother, he does not love me any more. I am sure he doesn't. I tried it with a daisy and it came out that way! *'Loves me, loves me not'* . . . and he *doesn't* love me!"

Grownups are often just as foolish. Not quite so frankly but quite as definitely they test God's love in similar ways.

It is usually testing God by daisy petals that makes his existence or his love uncertain. We establish standards of treatment which God may be expected to give us—so much happiness, so many years of life, so large a measure of success—and when these fail we can no longer be sure of God's love. Surely, we say, if there were a God, we would not be having these experiences; but there is no denying our experiences, and therefore there can be no God, or else he does not love us.

When war comes, there are men who say that God could have prevented the war, yet the war came; therefore there is no such God as they had supposed. It is only later that it is plain that with a just and loving God a war was inevitable while men lived as they did. We cannot sow dragon's teeth and reap peace. For thoughtful men God seems to emerge from the shadow where he has been keeping watch above his own laws and principles of human life. In the short view of history the great Avenger seems careless, unloving, indifferent to human needs and desires, but with the passing of the years the righteousness and love of God appear unmistakably.

In personal experience it is difficult to wait for the processes of life to work out. So often we settle down on some one isolated experience, refusing to look largely on life or even to see that single experience in its setting.

The maintenance of great forces which make all life possible, the daily care of the universe, the multitude of common every-day experiences which reveal someone's watchful care—all these get blotted from our sight by an adverse experience which at the very most we do not yet understand but which we know might prove one of God's great benedictions to us when it is fully worked out. So we pluck the petals of our daisy and find that God does not love us.

Seeing with Fresh Eyes

IT WOULD be a godsend to many of us if we could find a way of seeing the commonplace things of our lives with fresh eyes. A missionary said he sometimes wished he had never heard of Christ, so that he might have the delightful surprise that he saw in the faces of men when they were first told the story of the gospel. The gospel is always "good," but it is no longer "news" to a great many people.

The best way open to us to see with fresh eyes is through the eyes of others to whom they are fresh.

Most of us who are used to America have lost our sense of the marvel of all that is about us. Our vision may even be chiefly of the adverse facts. We are thinking of graft, lawlessness, and all the rest that is evil. After all is said, this continues to be the land of opportunity, the land of promise, and not of broken promise either. Here are still the largest liberties the world knows. Here is a chance for a new beginning. Education, art, culture, comfort, all are available for common people beyond the dreams of many in other lands.

Mary Antin tells in one of her books of the thrill that came to her after her arrival in this country, when a little girl, poorly dressed, invited her to go to school with her. When she asked what she would have to do to go, her new friend told her that she would need to do nothing but just come along. It was "incredibly glorious news." She saw with fresh eyes what is commonplace to us who live here.

The point for us is that we must shake ourselves out of the

dullness of the habit of such fine things. Our religion, our church, our land are all nothing short of marvelous. They are gloriously incredible. All it will take to make us realize that is to see with fresh eyes. We may need to bring ourselves to a new angle of vision.

It is an overwhelming pity that we should ever handle God's gifts with no thrill from the use of them.

> *My God, how endless is Thy love!*
> *Thy gifts are every evening new;*
> *And morning mercies from above*
> *Gently distill like early dew.*
>
> *I yield my powers to Thy command,*
> *To Thee I consecrate my days;*
> *Perpetual blessings from Thy hand*
> *Demand perpetual songs of praise.*

The Advantage of Strength

It is wise to center attention on young men and women in these days. Some of them are weak and need care, but the strong ones most need real care. It is their decisions that will count; it is their life choices that will mean most to others.

Strong men are the dangerous ones. They are the ones whose wreck would be greatest. A handcar can run off a railroad track with only slight damage, but a locomotive cannot leap the track without serious damage.

If any young man feels that he is strong, let him remember that therein lies his danger and his responsibility. To have power and to waste it or to misuse it is worse than failure without power.

One day an elderly man came to Dante Gabriel Rossetti with some sketches on which he wanted a judgment. Were they valuable? Could he hope to succeed as an artist? Rossetti was tenderhearted, and it hurt him greatly to have to say to the old man that his drawings were worthless and showed no promise. Then the old man laid before him some sketches done by a student. As Rossetti examined them he grew enthusiastic; he declared that the young man who drew them should be encouraged in every way. The old man was much moved, and exclaimed, "Ah, sir, I was that student!"

Great power had gone to waste. Promise had failed of fulfillment.

Unlikely men sometimes stride far ahead of men who set out most favorably. It is not that the strong men have always some fatal weakness; it is that they do not feel the burden of strength, but only the power of it.

The outstanding advantage of strength in young men and women is that the enterprise to which they are called needs strength. Strong hands are laying it down year by year. Strong hands must take it up.

Let there be no confusion about the enterprise. It is not preaching nor foreign missions. It is the whole matter of the purpose of Christ to found and extend his kingdom. It needs merchants and lawyers and doctors and homemakers, and all other kinds of people, as well as ministers and missionaries. There is room for everybody, and use for everybody, but there is largest need for the men who are strong.

The first appeal to strong men is not for this or that kind of work, but for a wholesale committal of themselves to Christ and his purpose. When that is finally settled, so that life is read in terms of Christ and his will, then the Spirit of God can possess and guide any life.

God can use weak men, but when he makes a strong man, it must be because such a man is peculiarly worthy of a great task.

The Ministry of Correspondence

WE READ recently that letter writing is a lost art. If that puts it too strongly, it is not too much to say that few men seem to realize its value as a means of service. People who feel the narrowness of their lives and wish for some larger opportunity of service might well consider whether they are not neglecting one of the largest opportunities which can come to anyone. A letter is an extension of one's personal influence into a wider circle. Some write too copiously, some write idly, some write triflingly in the effort to be interesting. But that means that the matter is not taken as a real opportunity for service.

Some of the busiest people have made of correspondence a ministry. Dr. J. R. Miller was a very busy city pastor, yet he found and made time for a correspondence which showed no signs of haste or carelessness or of mere chattiness. He wrote notes of cheer and comfort and gratitude and encouragement. His letters were not all "answers." He had none of that zeal for give-and-take which marks so many of us. He did not write letters in order to receive letters. And he often wrote to people whom he had never seen. Sometimes he read or heard tell of someone's experience which revealed a need for the fellowship which he himself felt with all men and which a letter could express.

How he found time for it in his busy life was always a mystery to his friends, but we can generally find time in the busiest life for doing what we count most important.

The fact is that most of the letters written today are not really worth while, but that many of them could easily be made worth while. They need only to be taken seriously by the one who writes them. A letter is for one or, at most, for a narrow circle of people. As though to show us how important individuals are, our Lord spoke his two most profound sentences to one woman, and one man, rather than to the crowd. "God is a Spirit," he told the woman at the well. "Ye must be born again," he said to Nicodemus.

Most of us will have to acknowledge that the purely physical labor of adequate writing hinders our effective use of this form of ministry. We do much less personally than our fathers had to do. We use typewriters, and it is amazing how few of us use them well. Or we dictate to a stenographer or to a machine, and few of us can keep the vital note when a third party is involved. Our handwriting becomes impossible.

Let all that be true. It remains that some of the largest ministry possible to us lies in letters. None of the difficulties is insurmountable. The "shut-in" can leave his room by means of them. The restricted life can be enlarged by them. The overburdened life can take on new ministry of helpfulness by them. Loads can be lifted by them. Hearts can be comforted by them. It is ministry so well worth rendering that it is worth while to render it well.

Morning Trust and Evening Trust

WHEN is it easier to feel confidence in God? In the morning or the evening?

Daylight brings things out so that we can see them. Most of us are braver in the daytime. Yet there are many who dread the coming of the morning. The very fact that we can see things often adds to our fear. As for the night, we cannot see then, and what mysterious peril may walk unseen we can only guess. Night is the opportune time for crime, when men hope to be hidden while they do evil.

Yet faith reminds us that God is equally in the night and the day. "The darkness and the light are both alike to thee." Whether day trust or night trust is more difficult, we who believe in God have a right to both.

In the inner life, morning and evening follow each other quite as much as they do in the outer life. Which is easier—the trust of prosperity or of adversity? When is it easier to think of God—when we bask in the sunlight of his blessing or stumble in the darkness of lack of that blessing? For some of us one trust is easier and for some the other. There are men who forget God whenever they prosper, who are turned back to him when the night of adversity comes on. There are men who grope for God in the dark, who rise up to greet him joyously when the light comes again. Here also it is enough that, whether the trust of prosperity or the trust of adversity is easier, we have a right to both.

God never leaves his children alone. If in the glamour of the sunshine they sometimes see his blessing so plainly that they miss him; if they hide from God behind the trees of the garden which he has given them, they need only to remember that all the sunshine is from him and that all prosperity is his gift. No ingratitude is worse than that which quietly assumes all God's blessings and leaves him out of account.

And he never leaves us alone in the dark. Some of us will never learn the strength of the arm on which we lean until we stumble and find that that arm upholds us. He does not lead us in the dark always to remind us of himself, but there are lessons that we learn in the dark of the soul which we never learn at any other time.

Passengers on the *Baltic* on that voyage in 1910 when the *Republic* sank and its passengers were brought back by the *Baltic* will never forget how the great rescuing steamer sailed round and round after reaching the supposed location of the injured vessel, whistling dismally and poking its nose through the fog, trying to find the ship. All afternoon the search went on, and when the night came most of the passengers felt sinking hearts in the thought that now it would be impossible to bring rescue until the morning. That was their mistake, for as the night grew darker it became possible to see the lights of the doomed vessel, and presently that which could not be found in the foggy light of the day became clear in the darkness of the night. That is a parable of our own lives. The best rescuers know the meaning of the dark. The best helpers of their fellows know what evening trust is.

Can We Pray about Everything?

DR. H. CLAY TRUMBULL said once that when he lost his pencil he considered it his privilege to ask God to help him find it. One of our correspondents asks if she has a right to her girlhood faith that she can pray about the color of ribbon she puts on when she dresses in the morning. She has come to question whether that is not a petty and cheap form of faith.

It is an old problem. Plato answered it by saying that the gods cared for the large but not for the small things. Solomon answers it by a code of principles, and says the small things are part of the concern of God in so far as they touch or express these principles of life.

Jesus deals with it more directly in his familiar saying that the hairs of our heads are all numbered in God's sight and that a sparrow cannot fall to the ground without the Father's notice. That would indicate that things which seem to us very slight are matters of concern to God. Jesus taught us about God that he is our Father and takes the attitude toward our interests that a father would naturally take toward the interests of his children. As long as something is important to a child it is important to the child's father or his mother.

A broken doll or a bruised finger is not much in itself to a father, but if it is a thing of deep concern to a child, the father cares on that account. The time may come when the father will wish that the child did not count these things as important, and he may feel that the child overemphasizes them. But he will always want his child to bring to him anything that really concerns him, assured that he will find concern in the father's heart. There is a stage in development when the formerly important things become incidental and can be treated so, but until they become incidental in the child's thought they are not incidental in the father's thought.

Dr. Trumbull's pencil was important to him; therefore it was important to the Father. Just as long as the color of her ribbons is important to our friend, she may feel sure she has a right to pray about it. The question which she must answer is whether it ought still to be important to her, whether it ought not now to be counted one of the incidental facts of life which God guards for her daily by reason of the committal of her life to him. It is important to God not because he loves ribbons but because he loves her and cares about anything that she cares about.

Slipping up the Alphabet

AN EXPERIENCED teacher advised his younger friends to be very simple in their teaching, to remember that their pupils did not know a great many things which they themselves could take for granted. "Remember," he said, "that many things that are A B C to you are X Y Z to others."

It is the teacher's business to make X Y Z facts become A B C facts. He is helped by the fact that everything tends to pass from strangeness to familiarity. It is one of the blessings of God that this is so, though, like all blessings, it involves a certain amount of danger. The danger is that we may allow great facts, which should always have for us an element of mystery, to become coolly commonplace to us.

People always tend to slip up the alphabet. Here you are with your circle of friends. Once their faces, their names, their manner of life were strange to you. Now they have become familiar. You can hardly think of yourself as being without them. Of course we are never intended to exhaust the meaning of our friends. There is always an element of the X Y Z in them. But it is a great blessing that people can grow so familiar to us that, while they retain an element of the unknown, we can hold them fast by what we do know.

Possessions take the same course. The luxuries of one generation are the commonplaces of the next and the absolute necessities of the third. Some of us can remember when business houses in New York City included in their newspaper advertisements that they had telephones, as proof of their progressiveness. The luxury of telephones has passed into a necessity. It is so with electric light and with all other so-called "modern improvements."

Ideas tend to take the same course. At first they are so offensive as to seem revolutionary. They are opposed tooth and nail. After a while they begin to look familiar. Gradually they no longer awaken any resentment. Finally they are accepted as commonplace facts. It would be impossible to make Galileo's theory a novelty before an audience today. It has slipped from the bottom to the top of the alphabet.

Did not Jesus mean that he himself would want to take that same course with us? He was not willing to call us servants and stand far away from us as a Master. He called us friends instead, because friends can know each other. There can never be full understanding of his greatness and power, but certainly we come to know more and to feel more familiar with the things of Christ as we come to know him better.

Has he passed from the unknown to the known in your life? Does he fit more into your everyday life, and does your everyday life take its form and direction more and more from him?

Big Talk and Small Deeds

MOST of us agree in big talk, in talk about things in the abstract, but it is hard to agree when the talk is brought down to some near-by application. When a small deed is to be performed, and the general principle is brought into play, we suddenly discover that there are good reasons in this particular instance why it should not apply.

Theological students tend to deal with people in the abstract. They study what they shall do in this emergency or that; how they shall present truth to "the sinner"; and how they shall deal with "the doubter." But of course there are no sinners or doubters in the abstract. They are always flesh-and-blood men, who refuse to allow either their sin or their doubt to be abstracted from the whole of their lives.

The same thing is true of churches. Any one of them can be handled properly in theory, but the difficulty is that there are always flesh-and-blood men in churches who want to have their own way, or at least refuse to fall into the ideal way which can be laid out. Big talk is easy, but small deeds are hard.

It is easy to declare that the way for churches to unite is to unite. Of course! Why not? All you have to do is just to bring the churches together. Say to people in an overchurched town, or an overchurched locality, "This division of yours is entirely wrong; you want to come together." Make their duty plain to them and see how readily you will heal the division in the body of Christ.

The only fault with that is that while its head is in the air its feet are not always on the ground. The people who make up these churches which are to be united so simply are just plain folks and they have their own ideas. They may agree with the abstract idea, but they usually want to apply it somewhere else. And it takes an immense amount of wisdom and tact and Christian grace to bring them to see in any single instance that the noble principles actually do apply in particular cases.

The same thing appears in the manifest Christian duty of helping the distressed. Who does not know that that is the business of us all? Do we not agree that the door of hope ought not to be shut in the face of an ex-convict; that a fallen woman who wants to come back to honor and social place ought to be welcomed in her effort? And yet how utterly abstract that ex-convict is, who is thought of in terms of the "ex-" and not in terms of flesh-and-blood men, with all the frailities he has brought with him. And the real trouble in helping fallen women back to their integrity is that they are not abstract at all, but are just women, with the faults and failings that go along with their history.

What all this comes to is not that we shall have less big talk but that we shall keep our big talk vital with small achievements, perpetually demanding that our theory be put into practice in the things that do lie at our hand.

Not less big talk but more small deeds.

The Selfishness of Parents

No HUMAN beings display year in and year out more of the beauty of unselfishness than parents. The burdens they bear for their children, the sacrifices they make for their welfare, the pains they endure for their good are beyond description or praise. Yet it is also true that there is no selfishness more galling and ruinous than that of selfish parents.

In earlier life, in the unselfish stage, they think of themselves in terms of their children. In later life they think often of their children in terms of themselves. Though the children are grown and responsible, these parents still wish to settle their life questions for them, and set up their own wishes as argument for a narrower life than children themselves want to live.

Their daughter gets a vision of the world field—sees it for herself alone, or for herself as the wife of a Christian man whose face is toward the mission field. She takes her wish to her father and mother, the very ones who ought to wish for her the largest, broadest life she can live. And they put their wishes squarely athwart her path. She must not go "so far away"; they would not think of letting her go to Japan or India, they might "never see her again." Sometimes they bid her choose between them and the young missionary or the foreign field. They tell her they would rather see her in her coffin than to have her go as a missionary.

We are not thinking now of non-Christian parents whose opposition is not surprising. We are thinking of Christian parents

94

who know what the meaning of the will of God is, in theory at least.

What parents say in such cases is that they love their daughter too much to let her go so far! They speak of it as a peculiar merit in themselves that, while other parents will let their children go away, they love their own so much that they cannot spare them. The plain fact is that they do not love their children deeply or truly enough to let them live their own lives. It is themselves they love. They are not asking what will be best for the child, whether it can be best for her to turn away from a purpose in which she is trying to do God's will. They put themselves in the place of God. The child must regulate her life by their desires.

There is hardly a hamlet in the land in which there are not limited, crippled lives, largely women's lives, denied their rightful chance because unwise parents selfishly demanded them when their real chance came. Daughters have been kept at home when the way ought to have been opened for their larger life, in homes of their own, in occupations or fields which they longed to enter.

It is all the fruit of plain, ugly selfishness, disguised in words of love. The part of parents is to fit children for life and then welcome the largest desires they have and set them free in every quest for the will of God and the widest service.

Using a Large Background

STANDING before a painting of Jean François Millet, a visitor remarked, "It always seems to me a long way to the back of one of Millet's pictures." That is an uncritical way of speaking of the background against which we see his figures. Something in us responds when figures in a painting are thrown against a large background. We see them better and understand them more clearly.

There is a principle of life involved here. The large background is needed to throw events and experiences into their right proportions. Troubles, for instance, are not cured by being seen against larger experiences, but they are made far more endurable. Some of us are egotists enough to feel that we are singled out for adverse treatment. No one ever had such pain as we have. No one ever had so many reverses. Our friends often see the absurdity of it but cannot often say what they think. A shrewd physician helped to cure a patient who was always complaining about her hard lot by taking her with him on a few afternoon rounds to homes where real trouble existed, letting her see her troubles against the larger background.

Often we need to see some part of our own experience against the whole background of God's dealing with us. Our troubles, our disappointments are items in a large total. They are details. They are not the whole of God's dealing with us. Our view of them must take into account our own conduct and the conduct of those with whom we are allied and whose consequences may fairly come upon us. It must consider the possible value of the experience to us in coming years.

In the matter of Christian beliefs we need a large background. At different periods or under differing experiences certain items of our faith come into prominence. We grow to be specialists in them. They tend to fill the field of vision and to seem all-important.

A large background is corrective for that evil. This important truth which we hold is not the whole of it. If we are fond of accent on the *sovereignty of God,* we see it in better proportion when we see also the *freedom of men.* If we rest joyously in the eternal *choice of God* to salvation, we hold it more safely when we realize also the demand for *acceptance by the chosen.*

Take further the matter of Christian service. It is possible to have such a high estimate of the importance of one particular piece of work that nothing else seems important. We condemn those who will not specialize on it. Or, on the other hand, we may lose the worth of some piece of service. We do not see it as part of the whole. What we can do is so little; why be careful of it? Then one day we see it in its place against a large background and it becomes essential. A clerkship becomes an element in the nation's commercial system. Ushering at the service becomes a part of the plan of the church for winning a whole community. Sunday-school teaching becomes a vital phase of the church's function as a teacher of truth.

The little matters can show great if the background is large.

The Cross as a Throne

THE CROSS of Christ makes a marvelous and varied appeal to men. There are many books about it. Men who talk of it, either from theory or from personal experience of its meaning, use widely varying language. No one phrase describes it.

But one conception of the cross, which is not so familiar as some others, is that the cross is a throne from which Christ is ruling. One of the early church fathers, speaking of it, said, "God is reigning from the tree!" It is a profound observation.

The cross is a throne of God's revelation. The heavens do not declare his *glory* more than the cross; the firmament does not show his *handiwork* more fully than the cross. Neither the heavens nor the firmament nor the earth reveals his *love* as does the cross. More men have been drawn to God by what they have seen of him as he is revealed in the cross than by all other manifestations together. Men have known him as God more fully there than anywhere else. It is there that he has flashed out his glory until men who have seen it have bowed in worship and have said, God is here.

The cross is also the throne of grace. Its arms have been stretched out to enclose the world, and from it Christ has ruled the hearts of men as in no other way. The surest note which our Lord ever sounded of his conquest is connected with his cross: "And I, if I be lifted up from the earth, will draw all men unto me." He said this about his death. It has not been chiefly the teaching of our Lord, and not even his resurrection glory, which have made him winsome and proved to men the abounding grace of God. It has been his cross.

In the nature of the case the cross becomes also a throne of judgment. It is sin which ruins men, but sin never looks so sinful as in the light of the cross. The final judgment is based on the sin of men, but the word of condemnation is to be for the rejection of the grace which is revealed in the cross. It is the cross which makes selfishness seem condemnable as it is. Measured by any other standard it does not seem so hideous. The cross is like a great flare of light that comes in the midst of darkness; it makes no evil, but shows what evil is already lurking there.

In the cross Christ condemned sin and of necessity condemned the man who so loves the sin that he will not turn from it. The cross must be a throne of judgment if it is also a throne of revelation and of grace.

> *When I survey the wondrous cross*
> *On which the Prince of Glory died*
> *My richest gain I count but loss*
> *And pour contempt on all my pride.*
>
> *Were the whole realm of nature mine*
> *That were a present far too small.*
> *Love so amazing, so divine,*
> *Demands my soul, my life, my all.*

The Chance for Heroism

STORIES of heroism always stir something in men's hearts. Probably there are circumstances in which any one of us would be a hero. We might miss many such chances, afraid of ourselves or blinded by more obvious unheroic results of the deed, but generally when men hear of a heroic deed something in them says, "I would have done that, too, if I had had the chance," or else, "Alas, that I haven't it in me to do that."

All this presupposes, however, that heroism consists in meeting bravely the exceptional opportunity. But what if there are none of these opportunities? What if life is just one long, unemotional grind, where nothing ever happens but the thing that happened yesterday and the day before that? What, indeed, if one's line of service is so completely secondary that great achievements are virtually impossible?

Young ministers want to be "out where the fight is strong, to be where the heaviest troops belong, and to fight there for God and man." They have had thoughts of taking their lives in their hands, making great sacrifices, and all that. And they find themselves in some village where they meet stolid indifference, where none of the evils of the times appears in definite enough shape to be fought, where everything they propose is accepted as a matter of course, where life is pleasant and easy. Here there seems no chance for heroism. The mere task of keeping the church going absorbs energy and time. The vision splendid fades.

A young woman hears the call to the heroic in college or at a convention, and her heart responds. She is ready for anything, eager for the most difficult thing. And then she finds herself buried in a round of prosaic schoolteaching or housekeeping in a little place, or writing letters in a business office all day until there is no power left for anything else. Nothing happens to her to break the monotony of life. She would willingly give her life for some great need, but she cannot get out from under the commonplace load she has to bear.

There is no need to multiply instances. The majority of men and women live in similar conditions. That is itself one of the great facts to be taken into account. If heroism were the lot of exceptional people only, then most people could not be heroic. But heroism does not belong to the few. There is a heroism of the commonplace, a way of illuminating drab and ordinary life.

Christ is the world's hero, yet his life was lived under most unheroic conditions. It was drab in itself except for the light which his own spirit threw on it and the beauty which shone on it from above. His circle was narrow, his occupations were uninspiring, his possessions meager, his visible results small and discouraging. Yet he lived a radiant life in the midst of it. It was the Father's plan for his life, and all his surroundings were, for him, shot through with beauty by that consciousness.

Helping a sick man here, comforting a sorrowing person there, teaching a handful of people now, making a talking trip then—all this does not sound like much, and many of his people are able to do much more imposing things. But when anything is part of a plan of the Father, and when it leads on to the saving of men, who can want to do anything better? And when Christ was leaving his message for men he told them to be lights, set for daily shining. He left no impossible tasks for anybody. He left instead a duty of daily life which gives the best in men its full chance. Shining, savoring, blessing one's own place—he left that for everyone. For himself he found beauty in such a life. Others will find the chance for daily heroism where he found it.

The heroic element gets into life also by way of fellowship with those who are doing the exceptional thing. Campbell Morgan says rightly that "for the ordinary church member or Christian worker or minister, life in the mission field would be almost insupportable." But that life would be impossible for the missionaries if people of the more commonplace life here did not make it possible. It is something to live the kind of life that makes heroism possible in other lives. It may be the man who is lowered into the dark pit who is the hero of the rescue, but it is something to have had a hand on the rope which held him while he went down. These heroes are part of the brotherhood. Their spirit is the outcome of many lives. When a man takes the heroic into his fellowship he gets some of the values for himself.

Each man must know that no life is permanently shut out from heroism. Each life has its chance to be great.

Loyalty to Truth: Loyalty to a Truth

THOSE look like the same thing, but they are a long way from being the same. One is big, and the other can be the littlest thing imaginable. Being loyal to a truth may leave one a pinhead thinker. Loyalty to truth will always make one broad-souled and strong. Some critics have a fondness for indicating a great man's "central truth." It is a thankless task, for it cannot be done in any final way. Great men rejoice in truth of all sorts and kinds. They do not know what you mean by being loyal to a truth, as though it could be held by itself. They hold all truths as parts of the truth.

Just push anything as though it were the whole truth and it lands you in an absurd position. Make a hobby of any truth and you ride off a precipice. The average man who goes wrong in belief does it when he forgets that there are other truths besides his favorite one. What we mean by religious fads always have at the heart of them something which is genuine and necessary and desirable. The various fancies of the day are lopsided truths which need the contact of other truths to straighten them up. The trouble generally is that the truth they involve has been neglected and in the joy of its rediscovery it is treated as though it were the only truth alive.

You can see that in any convention of believers who come together around some particular item of faith. They all fall into the most extravagant modes of speech; they become sharply critical of people who differ from them; they magnify this particular matter of faith into first and even final importance. "Accept this, and accept it as we do," they say, "or show yourself disloyal to the truth of God." They are sure all wise men agree about it. Disagreement is a proof of lack of wisdom. They are not so much concerned about truth as about a truth.

There are at least three bad effects of being so devoted to a truth that one cannot see it as part of the truth.

One is a tendency to distort that truth until it is found overshadowing all others. You catch that in the enthusiastic way in which the advocates of some particular truth assure us that it is the key to a large variety of problems. Acceptance of it, they say, explains the power of the church in all powerful periods; denial is the reason for all times of weakness. No matter what truth it is, the man who is a specialist in it is perfectly clear that it lies at the foundation of everything else. He counts the number of times it occurs in the Bible or early church documents. He can take a parable of our Lord and show it there with an amazing ingenuity. Presently everything else becomes subsidiary to that one truth. It is not to be tested by anything; everything is to be tested by it. In his passion for a truth, the believer has lost his sense of truth.

A second bad effect of loyalty to a truth instead of to truth is a tendency to dwarf other phases of truth. In an inquiry from a church committee for a new minister the clause occurred: The only demand we make about his preaching is that he let up on a certain doctrine, for if we do not know all about it by this time, we are hopeless; our former pastor gave us little else. The church had been overfed on one doctrine, and thereby underfed on others. A young minister expected praise from an older one when he declared that for a whole year he had been hammering away at one truth, but the wiser one could only tell him that by this time it was probably battered beyond recognition and had better be left alone in the interest of the whole truth.

A third bad effect of loyalty merely to a truth is the tendency to arouse a critical spirit against those who do not hold it in the same way or who accent something else. Among brethren this is worst of all. As men go to extremes on any item of faith they become suspicious of their fellows who are not ready to go with them. They think others must be disloyal to Christ, or stupidly ignorant, or willingly indifferent. So they say contemptuous words about ministers or teachers who do not hold the same view. It is no longer a matter of opinion, no more a matter of interpretation; it is a matter of honesty, of fairness, of real religion. So they pass into a carping, critical spirit, which sees all others in error and only themselves right. Thus the truth becomes not winsome and beautiful but restrictive and discredited, and the friends of the truth become unwittingly its enemies. They could have saved it all by seeing each truth as part of the truth and practicing a deep loyalty to the whole.

Troubled by the Entrance of Christ

"When Herod the King heard it, he was troubled." The news of Christ's coming is the best news the world ever had, but it troubles some people who hear it. Herod totally misunderstood it. If there were to be a new "king of the Jews" it meant a change in the conditions which Herod was used to. It meant loss and harm to himself and the encouragement of impossible desires among the people. The larger beneficent meanings did not occur to Herod, of course. It would have seemed to him the sheerest nonsense that, in coming centuries, his own greatest claim to fame would be that Christ came during his reign. That the disturbing Christ would be rather the world's Prince of Peace would have been incredible to Herod.

When Jesus healed the demoniac and permitted the destruction of the swine, he had done a good work in setting a man free. That was beyond discussion. But still, there were the swine! Christ had disturbed the existing order, and there were not a few who besought him that he would depart out of their coasts. Their minds were altogether fixed on the adverse meanings of his presence.

Things can never be left as they have been when Christ comes into any life or any enterprise. If there are not great changes when he enters, it is because he is not given his place. The shame of the church for centuries past is that he has not been allowed to make the difference he should have made. Herod's misunderstanding was nearer the truth than a placid acceptance of Christ and a demand that he leave bad conditions unchanged.

A bit of grim humor gets into a church order of service occasionally if, when Miss Havergal's hymn is scheduled, only the first line is printed: "Take my life and let it be...." That is exactly what Christ will not do. If he takes a life, he will not "let it be." Those who hesitate to give their lives to Christ for fear of what he may ask them to do are wise in stopping to consider, though their fear is wholly misplaced. It is quite certain he will do something with their lives that will make a tremendous difference with them. What he does will enrich and ennoble life, to be sure, but if they are so enamored of what they are that they cannot think happily of any change, then they cannot want Christ to come in.

There are similar adverse aspects of Christ's entrance into business or public life. Commercial competition may not be destroyed, but it must certainly be modified if the spirit of Christ comes to rule. Oppression of the poor and distressed, indifference to the rights of employees or employers, exploiting of women for pleasure and of children for profit and of men for dividends will necessarily be arrested if Christ comes in.

The same disturbance will come when Christ enters into international relations. Some pet ideas will be exploded. The hallucination that guns and ships make peace will blow away into the thin air of which it is made. There must disappear also the notion that love of one country involves hatred of another, that care for the interests of one land means disregard of the interests of another.

Jesus Christ cannot take hold of any life or any part of life and "let it be."

The Value of Being Nice

WE TRUST we have a healthy contempt for petty criticism which is willing to stake a man's character on some peccadillo of behavior. The proper use of the table napkin is not final evidence of a call to the ministry, and the overconspicuous use of a toothpick is not satisfactory evidence of unfitness for the pulpit.

It was said of a famous frontier preacher that if he got as much food into his mouth as had evidently been spilled on his once black coat it would have foundered him. If Mr. Spurgeon's coat ever really fitted him, the fact is not remembered by many of his hearers. Yet both the frontier preacher and Mr. Spurgeon could outpreach most of the perfectly proper gentlemen who criticised them. Jesus hints in his word about John the Baptist that he was not arrayed for the palace, but he shook palaces just the same. Power does not lie in these things, but at far deeper levels of reality.

For all that, there is distinct value in being nice. The value evaporates when niceness becomes mere foppishness, and fear of that sad outcome is sometimes the excuse which men have for being crude and rough and negligent. Because there is no spiritual grace in a clean collar or carefully combed hair, some men go upon the supposition that there is such grace in a soiled collar or tousled locks. All this is too bad, for it is really worth while in the interest of the gospel to be nice.

An entering class in Princeton Theological Seminary some years ago was advised by President Patton to "pray without ceasing and shave every morning." Praying without ceasing takes care of the springs of power, but a daily shave helps to maintain outward evidence of inward grace.

We are prepared to affirm, after some experience, that whereas no man ever gained power by negligence, many a man has lost power by it. There are always enough people to whom such things matter to make it worth any man's while to regard them, if he cares to influence those people. In the poorest home of a large parish we once heard a humble woman praise her minister because he was always such a gentleman when he came into her cheap and cramped abode that she wanted to make the place cleaner.

Paul urged young Timothy, "Let no man despise thy youth, but be thou an example to them that believe, in word, in manner of life, in love, in faith, in purity." There must be some hint of the niceties of behavior in that injunction about being an example in "manner of life." Certainly we lose nothing by being careful in our manner and appearance when we are representing the saving gospel of Christ.

Sunday as a Day for Thinking

How TO make the most of the Sabbath is a genuine puzzle to some good people.

There are four elements which go to make up the best-kept Sabbath. They are worship, work, fellowship and thinking. The characterizing element is doubtless the first, but manifestly all the hours of the day cannot be spent in distinctive acts of worship, unless the phrase is taken in a very wide sense. Yet worship must have a dominating place in a well-kept Sabbath.

Certainly, also, there ought to be some feature of service for others in the name of Christ. It may be a Sunday-school class, a visit to a sick friend, a service of comfort and cheer, participation in the organized work of the church in some form, or any one of a dozen bits of work. Such work is proper keeping of the Sabbath.

The Sabbath is also a day for fellowship, for families and for friends who know and are known. It is not the day for general social gatherings—teas, parties, frankly secular meetings at the homes of friends, but opposition to these must not blind us to the value of the day for meeting our friends in true Christian fellowship. It is a day for families to have at the dinner table young men and women whose homes are far away. It is the day for children to be in the grandparents' home. It is a day for reading or talk that is cheering and helpful.

There remains the most neglected of the uses of the day. The Sabbath is the ideal day for thinking. Men sometimes wondered that Mr. Gladstone could do so much religious writing when the subject lay so far from his political field. He told the secret of it himself. He kept his Sabbaths for religious thinking. He had some lines of reading and thought reserved for that day. This served also to keep his mind off the pressing problems which might follow him to the late hours of Saturday. When Sunday came he had his place of worship, his share of work, his chance at fellowship and his line of thought. Thus he came back to his task of Monday refreshed.

For most of us the seed of the thinking of the day would naturally be some part of the Scripture. We dip into the Bible during the week, but Sunday brings our chance to go over a new part or over an old part in a new way and to do it carefully. Some of us, to tell the truth, have grown tired of the Bible. We have exhausted the surface veins, and we must strike the deeper ones. Sometimes we can do that best by using an unfamiliar version, or a commentary or a biblical introduction. Ask a minister for counsel.

We ought also to keep on hand some strong books for Sunday reading. Most of us do not spend money enough for good religious books. Here is our chance. Let us do a bit of honest, downright thinking on the Sabbath, enriching our souls with truth and keeping our minds from the things that crowd them all through the week.

What Can Plain People Do about It?

SOME of us are glad we are not just now the President of the United States. Others of us seem to wish we were, because then we would do such wonderful things in the crisis of nations which is on. But none of us is the President. We are just plain people with no visibly direct influence on the relations of nations. Is there anything we can do about it, then? Have we any duty about the large evils which we seem to see from afar, which we can feel, which we know ought to be cured and which we think could be cured but which we cannot reach directly or effectively? What can plain people do about large evils?

Take war itself as an illustration. Any war that will ever arise in the world, any war that ever has arisen, is the result of an atmosphere rather than of an event. Worse events than the ones that start the war have occurred over and over again, and nothing serious came from them. They were allowed to die out without strife. But this event happened in an atmosphere charged with explosive material. Exactly so a match goes out if it falls in the roadway, but does not go out if it is dropped in a wastebasket of loose paper.

Now the creation of an atmosphere is the work, in the largest part, of us plain people. We can refuse to be party to the creation of an atmosphere conducive to strife. We can be persistently brotherly. We can persistently refuse to think the worst of all other people in all other lands. We can have large ideas of brotherhood ourselves, and we can talk about them.

This is the way public opinion and the national atmosphere

come to be. Talking is the largest single factor in it. Personal conversations are weightier than editorials. What men say to each other at lunch, and what women say to each other in their social gatherings, have actually more weight and are more commonly quoted than what they read in their papers.

Specially is it true in a democracy that talk is a large factor in public life. It creates the atmosphere in which public men can do things, the atmosphere in which, at times, they are forced to do things.

All great movements, all great national experiences are first of all the theme of the talk of the common people. Thus they become matters of course. Every time we talk boastfully in private conversations of what we must do in order to be ready to fight other nations, we help to make an atmosphere in which fighting other nations becomes easy. Whenever we join the chorus of thoughtless men who minimize the value of international brotherhood, we help to loosen the ties of that brotherhood.

We plain people, getting clear ideas ourselves and expressing them freely, make the conduct of our leaders more certain than anything they can do themselves.

"An Hearty Desire To Pray"

AN OLD prayer from the Gregorian sacramentary runs in this way: "And grant that we to whom thou hast given an hearty desire to pray may by thy mighty aid be defended and comforted in all dangers and adversities."

The central clause sticks in one's memory. So often we question whether we need to pray or whether there can be any use in prayer. Such questions and objections drop away when we have a sufficiently "hearty desire to pray." We can all find good reasons for doing what we genuinely want to.

There are three feelings that move us to prayer.

The first is a strong sense of *obligation to pray*. The command is plain. We are not advised nor recommended to present our petitions to God; we are explicitly told to do so. In the lives of most men comes the time when that sense of obligation tides them over the weakening of their spiritual enthusiasm. They ought to pray. They may not be clear about the results nor the theory of it, but they cannot get away from the feeling that a dependent creature owes it to God, on whom he depends, to present humbly his petitions and his submissions.

Secondly, in the lives of many of us there is a deep sense of the *need to pray*. We feel about it as has been said about the sense of God: "If there were no God, it would be necessary to invent one." The sense of need to pray is deepest in times of great burdens or distresses, but no one who has the habit of prayer can fail to realize the deepening sense of his need for prayer. He cannot keep his heart light without it; he cannot keep his hands strong without it; he cannot keep his head clear without it. It appears in every great emergency in life; everybody prays when the ship is about to sink.

There is, however, a third feeling in many hearts: the feeling of a joyous sense of the *right to pray*. When Dr. Charles E. Jefferson was a young man planning to go into the ministry, he went to see Phillips Brooks and asked him if, as a Christian, he was compelled to believe in the miracles. Dr. Brooks replied, "I should not say that you are compelled to do so; I should say that you may do so!" Dr. Jefferson said that this made a change in his whole outlook upon the miracles.

We have a right to pray. This is sure. Having such a God as we have, with such love as he feels, no laws of nature and no fixed purpose could possibly take from us the right to come into close fellowship with him. We are at our best when we feel "an hearty desire to pray."

Professor Knight has given us a beautiful prayer which many of us may use in our time of weakening in prayer:

> O Thou who has taught us to continue patient
> in well-doing, and dost assure us that in due
> time we shall reap if we faint not, help us
> to welcome whatsoever thou ordainest; and
> though our road wind uphill all the way, may
> we persevere to the end, through Jesus
> Christ our Lord. Amen.

Is Thy God Able?

AFTER a sleepless night the king comes to the mouth of the den of lions to see whether Daniel has been protected. Evidently he feels that the one under test is not Daniel, but Daniel's God. Daniel has made a great point of his relation to God, and has allowed it to distinguish his life from others. Now came a test, not of Daniel but of his God. So the question of the king is not "Are you alive? Have you survived?" but "Is thy God able to deliver thee?"

That is the cry of the world still. "You say you believe in God. You talk bravely about his power. Here are trying experiences, sorrow, hardship, calamity: Does your faith count now? Is thy God able?"

When men without the Christian faith see believers break and fail and fall, see them devoured by the lions of sorrow or adversity or even of sin, the world does not stop with condemning them. It goes on to declare there is nothing in what they believe, after all. The world persistently measures God by the men who claim to believe in him. So it becomes immensely important that men have such thought of God as sustains them in their adverse experiences. Is God as we know him really able to do what needs to be done in our lives?

Here are great advances in science. What do they do to your faith? Do you tremble for the future? Is thy God able? The real, triumphant faith welcomes all these new discoveries in the assurance that every one that is finally proved true will bring more glory to God, will make the Christian revelation so much the more beautiful; and every one that is not true will soon be disproved. Our God is able! Our Christ is equal to all the strain of all the new knowledge that can be found! It will all yet be a diadem of glory for him.

Here are great social evils. They flaunt themselves in the face of society, or they skulk in dark places and wait to strike the social order in time of peril. Do you despair? Do you give up? Do you fight on in a dogged, hopeless fashion? Do you feel that they cannot be ended, that they are here to stay? Or is thy God able? Has humanity actually got the upper hand of your God, so that no matter how loyally his people serve him he and they are yet to be defeated? Is that the kind of God you are trusting?

Here is your personal life, with all its struggles and defeats and failures. That old habit of yours—are you never to conquer it? That temperamental defect of yours—is it never to be made good? Is thy God able?

Three great texts which speak of the ability of God ought to come with great comfort to us in our personal lives. One is in Hebrews (7:25): "He is able to save to the uttermost them that draw near unto God through him." So his ability meets us at the entrance to the Christian life. Then another Hebrews verse (2:18): "In that he himself hath suffered being tempted, he is able to succor them that are tempted." His ability goes with us on the way. And finally, the verse with which Jude closes his epistle: "Unto him that is able to guard you from stumbling and to set you before the presence of his glory without blemish in exceeding joy." His ability carries the work through to completion.

Is thy God able? *Is thy God able?*

The Song in the Night

IT MUST not be forgotten that the first Christmas song was sung in the night. The glory broke over the world when the world was dark. "There were shepherds abiding in the fields, keeping watch over their flocks by night." And it was into one of the dark corners of the earth that the light came. In little, obscure Judea, near little, obscure Bethlehem—there the world's Light shone for the first time; there the angels sang.

That is a comforting fact. When the world is dark, the light shines, not from among men but from heaven, and what it shows is not a marching host of Herod's men insuring peace, but a Prince of Peace who seeks his mastery in men's hearts. Peace has to be made and kept in the heart. We must find our way to a manger before we pass out of the dark of the night.

And that is specially true in personal lives. Never a Christmas comes that is not a mockery in some homes. The year has brought its sorrows, its losses, its reverses. "Merry Christmas," people say: how can they be so simple as to think that any day can be merry again? The world is dark. And, indeed, human songs seem trifling at such times, and human lights seem dim and unreal. But the night need not be unbroken and the waiting need not be silent. Heaven still arches over earth, and the angels can still sing of peace of heart to men who are of good will.

For the Christmas assurance supremely is that God has not forgotten human need. Christ did not come when he was expected nor as he was expected. Nor did he come to do what men expected he would do. He came to meet the deepest need men have and to meet it according to a plan far higher than their wisdom would have suggested. God had not forgotten. Nor has he forgotten now. On the Judean throne was an impossible king; in Rome was one who was little better. And here in Bethlehem is born a Babe—to deal with such a situation!

But after all, that is the way in which God has shown himself at work before and since. His plans run far. They start where they are least expected to begin. They take hold on the least accepted instruments. They are announced first where it was not to be supposed they would be known. But they move by the most effective paths after all. It is a slow process, terribly slow, this method of bringing peace to the world and to the human heart, but it moves on effectively once it is under way. God's method gives assurance of permanence. It begins with a Babe and it goes on by way of a cross, but it has a resurrection, an ascension and a Pentecost.

If, therefore, at the Christmas season it seems a travesty to think of being merry, at least the heart can listen for a song in the night which will tell that God's angels are there, and he is remembering.

Making up One's Mind to It

EVEN the greatest people can be a bit foolish at times. When Margaret Fuller declared resignedly that she accepted the universe, Carlyle was quite right in snarling that she'd better. One does not quite see what Margaret Fuller would have done if she had decided not to accept the universe. The limits of feasible rebellion are narrow for us all.

Who gets the damage if we decide we will not accept the universe? The universe has the most provoking way of going on about its business in spite of us. Continuing to struggle against inevitable conditions brings us only unhappiness. Birds that go on living in a cage are the ones that cease flinging themselves against the bars. It may look heroic to kill oneself flying against the cage bars, but it serves no real purpose. When we find out what the universe about us really is, the time has come to accept it and to learn to be happy in it. It may be a universe of disappointment and lost hopes and a great deal else that is unpleasant and unfortunate, but if it is really inevitable, the only course is to make up one's mind to it and then to take it as it actually is.

That is one side of a great truth. Left to itself, however, it might be a most dangerous truth. There are things in the universe which are no real part of it. They are there because no one has had the energy to put them out, or to put better things in their place. It is always easier to let evils alone. It is always comforting to say that evils are rooted in the nature of things, so that there is no use in trying to change them.

A dirty city is always easier to have than a clean one. A dwindling church is always less costly than a growing one. It takes less work to neglect a church roll and let its members play fast and loose with church obligation than to stiffen up the meaning of church membership. We talk in church meetings of the "conditions of the times" and declare piously that we have determined simply to do our duty and leave the results to God—meaning that we have accepted a negligent church and vacant pews.

Well, one thing is sure: the people who have made up their minds to such things are not the ones who get anything done to correct them. Florence Nightingale put us in her debt by her refusal to make up her mind to the wrong things. She encountered her largest trouble in the people who had made up their minds to the evils she set out to correct. They were people who had become happy little birds in cages whose doors would readily have swung open if they had pushed. Not finding the doors, they had stopped pushing and were eating crackers of content. Florence Nightingale could not believe there were no doors. She beat against the bars until they proved to be doors into larger freedom for all.

In such people lies the hope for the world. The universe is not altogether as God meant it to be. We are here partly to change it. One of his mercies is that as men grow older and used to things, he takes them away and puts the universe in the hands of young, fresh men. When the young man comes into responsibility, the older ones shake their heads and wonder how soon he will learn from experience. The real hope is that he will not learn some things from experience at all but will refuse to believe them.

Young or old, we must not make up our minds to things unless we know they are God's things.

Truths That Counterbalance

TWO OPPOSITE forces are at work on our planet. One of them would draw it into the sun and so to its ruin; the other would thrust it away from the sun and hurl it forth to utter destruction. Either force by itself would be calamitous. Together they keep the world in its orbit.

Either one of a pair of truths in religion may be disastrous to faith, while the counterbalance of the two will be saving in power.

There is the fact of the nearness of God, what the books call his *immanence*. Push it too far and you have *pantheism*— a God lost in the world to which he is so near. The two truths cherished together will hold believers in their orbit.

There is the fact of the greatness of God, over and above and through all the world, what the books call his *transcendence*. Push it too far and you have *deism*—an absentee God, as Carlyle said. Yet take the two together and you have the God and Father of our Lord Jesus Christ, closer to us than breathing and nearer than hands and feet, yet high in the heavens, to be approached with all boldness, yet with all reverence. When men become irreverent and familiar they have forgotten how great is God. When they feel themselves deserted they have forgotten his nearness. They need both truths together.

There is the fact of the *humanity* of Christ, his true unity with the human race. Push it too far and he is no longer God, and redemption is not the work of God but of man imitating Christ. There is the fact of the *deity* of Christ. Push it too far and he is no longer man but only an appearance, a kind of pretense, not a brother to the race who knows the life of men because he has lived it. Take the two great facts together. Count Christ true man and true God, God-man, and his salvation is both near and mighty.

One Christian belief is that followers of Christ are to be *separate from the world,* God's chosen, peculiar people. In some hands that becomes a plea for asceticism, for oddity, for refusal to enter into the life of society. On the other hand it is a matter of Christian belief that followers of Christ are the salt of the earth, lights set on candlesticks, cities which cannot be hid, and on this account they must *mingle with the world*. In some hands that is sheer worldliness. Not even the sharpest eye can detect the difference between some such believers and the most worldly unbeliever. If protest is made, you get familiar remarks about not liking "long-faced Christians," that "Christians ought to have a good time." Both phases of the truth, held in honesty and eagerness, are needed. The Christian will be in the world for the world's sake, not for his own. And he will drop all cheap talk about his own right to a good time when that compromises his testimony for Christ.

Possibly it is laymen who are most in danger from lack of balance. Stressing the doctrine of *God's love,* they sometimes fail to see the demand he makes on men for *righteousness* by reason of that very love. So they think the heathen are saved without the gospel. Accenting the fact of *human responsibility,* they underestimate the necessity for *divine grace*. Sure of the *fatherhood of God,* they neglect the *holiness of that fatherhood*.

But all truth carries its own safeguards to a heart eager for truth. The counterbalancing truth comes soon into sight if loyalty to truth is the first ambition of the soul.

123

God's Persistent Seven Thousand

And Ahab told Jezebel ... how he had slain all the prophets with the sword. Then Jezebel sent a messenger unto Elijah saying, So let the gods do to me, and more also, if I make not thy life as the life of one of them by tomorrow about this time. ... And Elijah went for his life and came unto a cave and lodged there. ... And he said to Jehovah, The children of Israel have forsaken thy covenant, thrown down thine altars, and slain thy prophets with the sword; and I, even I only, am left. ... And Jehovah said unto him ... Yet will I leave me seven thousand in Israel, all the knees which have not bowed unto Baal, and every mouth which hath not kissed him.—From I Kings 19.

WHAT with Jezebel's boasting that Jehovah's people had been destroyed, and Elijah's agreeing that they were, indeed, it must have been a bit hard for good people of that day to keep cheerful. The fact is that Jezebel took counsel of her hopes and Elijah of his fears, but neither of them took counsel of the facts. The seven thousand were there, but neither Jezebel nor Elijah saw them.

Meanwhile, if the seven thousand knew what the two were thinking or saying, they would have either been amused, which is not likely, or depressed, which is probable. Even if you know a thing is not so, it makes you restless to have high authority assert it confidently.

If you had lived in those times and had read in the morning paper that Jezebel declared that the worship of Jehovah was losing ground, and virtually gone, and then had seen in the evening paper that Elijah admitted that Jezebel was right, observing that he was about the only worshiper left, you might have known better because you were one yourself, but it would have taken a little of the stiffening out of you.

If we listen too carefully to some people today, it takes loud whistling to keep up courage. But let us remember that everybody who has kept cheerful and sure of God in other ages has had to adopt the same course. One need only take down an old Butler's *Analogy* to read in its preface that in the middle of the eighteenth century "many persons" seemed agreed that Christianity was fictitious and was to be counted "a principal subject of mirth and ridicule." Later in the same century David Hume said, "Most people in England have divested themselves of all superstitious reverence for names and authority; the clergy have lost much of their credit, their pretensions and doctrines have been ridiculed, and even religion can scarcely support itself in the world."

When, therefore, we read today of men who take counsel of their hopes and declare that religion has less and less hold on men, and when our brethren take counsel of their fears and admit that it is certainly so, let us not grow too pale about it. Let us take counsel of the facts. God's seven thousand are wonderfully persistent. They keep emerging. Jezebel keeps killing them with swords or books or lectures, and Elijah keeps holding their obsequies and feeling his own solitariness. Meanwhile, yonder they are, all over the land, each doing his own part, and God knows and loves them, and under the right leadership they will assert themselves. Our business is to see that we belong to the number, and if Elijah and Jezebel sing their funeral duet too lugubriously, we might rise up and refuse to be buried.